Contents

World Folktales

Level 5

Retold by Kathy Burke
Series Editors: Andy Hopkins and Jocelyn Potter

Pearson Education Limited
Edinburgh Gate, Harlow,
Essex CM20 2JE, England
and Associated Companies throughout the world.

ISBN: 978-1-4058-6252-3

First published by Penguin Books 2003
This edition published 2008

1 3 5 7 9 10 8 6 4 2

Text copyright © Penguin Books Ltd 2003
This edition copyright © Pearson Education Ltd 2008
Illustrations by David Cuzik (Pennant Illustration)

Typeset by Graphicraft Ltd, Hong Kong
Set in 11/14pt Bembo
Printed in China
SWTC/01

Published by Pearson Education Ltd in association with
Penguin Books Ltd, both companies being subsidiaries of Pearson Plc

For a complete list of the titles available in the Penguin Readers series please write to your local
Pearson Longman office or to: Penguin Readers Marketing Department, Pearson Education,
Edinburgh Gate, Harlow, Essex CM20 2JE, England.

Introduction

Pieces of the evil light were everywhere. He saw them clearly, dancing around him, causing him to cough, giving him night fevers. ("Breaking the Chain")

Thiazi took Idun to Jotunheim, high in the mountains . . . Here he kept Idun prisoner so that, without the apples, the gods would grow old—but he would stay young forever. ("The Golden Apples")

In both these folktales evil has been done and a way to defeat it must be found. The first is a story from Guatemala, in which one bloody murder leads to another. Can Juanantes break the chain of violence? Or must it continue? The second is a Scandinavian tale set in the ice world of the gods. The kidnapper and thief is Thiazi, one of the giants who are the enemies of the gods. As the gods grow old they lose their minds and powers. Can they save themselves before it is too late?

In "Wisdom for Sale," less serious problems are solved by a poor orphan boy in his little shop in an Indian marketplace. He sells his advice to anyone who needs it, but the advice is so good that his customers include a merchant's son and even a king.

Magic and love bring both trouble and joy in "The Wooden Horse," an ancient tale from the Middle East. The wooden horse has been made by an old wizard and has very special qualities which take a young prince on some amazing adventures. The Russian whose mother throws him out of his home in "The Good Peasant's Son," because he has spent his last money on rescuing a dog and a cat instead of on buying food, also needs the help of magic to bring him a new life—and love.

"Lukas's Luck" is set in former Czechoslovakia, where winters are long and hard and farmers pray for the arrival of spring.

Like Martin, the young Russian, Lukas and his family have lost everything—they can't even find a godmother who will bring gifts for their baby. Is there any way out of their troubles?

Kindness and cruelty are important to many of the stories in this collection, but in the African tale "The Crocodile and the Hunter" men must live side by side with animals. Sometimes, in the wild, they depend on each other's help—but can they trust each other?

Two of the stories, "The Wedding Box" and "Happy New Year," describe the daily lives of people in ancient China. In the first story, a spoiled young woman learns to think of others, and not only of herself. In the second, a generous man gives away all his money and then has to find a way to enjoy a very disappointing New Year's holiday.

This is a collection of folktales from around the world. A folktale is a traditional story which has been passed down in spoken form, from person to person, often over hundreds of years. Every culture has its own folktales, and a large number have only been written down fairly recently. So the story we read or listen to today may be quite different from the original. Very often we have no idea who the original author was.

Folktales all over the world show great similarities. There is always a problem or difficulty that the hero or heroine must deal with. At the start we are told the time and place of the story, and the main character is introduced. Then the story develops with a problem or series of problems that the hero must find the answer to. The stories may be happy, sad, funny, wise, or exciting adventures, but there is usually an important lesson about life and relationships to be learned.

There are different kinds of folktales, but the same types are found in many cultures. The animal folktale is very common in African and South American countries. In earlier cultures, animals played an important part in people's lives, and in folktales they are often given human qualities and are able to talk to human beings. "The Crocodile and the Hunter" is a typical African animal folktale in which the crocodile is shown to be a murderous liar!

Another important type of folktale is one that tells a story about gods and goddesses. Although most cultures have such stories, in some cultures—in Ancient Greece, Ancient Rome, and India, for example—these gods and goddesses formed an important part of the culture's belief system or religion. The Scandinavian culture also has a strong tradition of such stories; "The Golden Apples" is a wonderful example of a Scandinavian god behaving badly and having to make things right again.

A third type of folktale, in some ways similar to stories of gods and goddesses, involves heroes or heroines with powers that are often magical. "The Wooden Horse," from the Middle East, is an example in this collection. These stories show man's desire to be more powerful than he really is, the impossible desire to have powers that are more than human. In the Middle East, the most ancient examples are the stories about Gilgamesh, a being who was two-thirds god and one-third man. These stories were recorded on pieces of stone as long ago as 3000 B.C.

Other types of stories involve more ordinary people, for example, merchants or simple peasants. "The Good Peasant's Son" and a number of other stories in this collection are of this type. If the folktale is about a peasant, it is often about how the hero becomes wealthy and marries well.

Magic plays an important part in many folktales. Often, the hero of the story finds, is given, or wins something that gives him magical powers, as in "The Good Peasant's Son". Or, the hero may meet someone, like an old woman, who has magical powers, as happens in "Lukas's Luck." The hero must then use this magical gift wisely. Magical powers are at their most important in fairy tales, stories that have very little connection with reality as we know it. "The Wooden Horse" is a typical Middle Eastern fairy tale.

The serious study of folktales only began in the nineteenth century, and Jacob and Wilhelm Grimm (the Brothers Grimm) are seen as the people who started the systematic study of "folk" stories. The two brothers collected German folktales from friends, relatives, and villagers. Between 1812 and 1822 they produced the three collections known as "Grimm's Fairy Tales," stories that are read to children today all over the western world.

Since then, serious efforts have been made in many countries to record folktales in written form. In 1890, A Scotsman called James Frazer wrote a book called "The Golden Bough." This widely-read and important book examines folktales in relation to religion, belief systems, and culture.

In the twentieth century, the American Joseph Campbell (1904–1987) was very important in the study of folktales. In his work, Campbell explored the many characters and storylines shared by folktales all over the world. Following the ideas of the psychologist Carl Jung, Campbell showed that in all traditional stories there are characters who appear regularly and represent universal characteristics in human society. These include the evil person, the helper (who guides the hero), and the character who plays tricks.

Campbell's work has had enormous importance in Hollywood, the home of American movies. George Lucas, the director of the extremely successful *Star Wars* films, made in the late 1970s and early 80s, based his ideas on Campbell's work—*Star Wars* is often described as a science fiction fairy tale. Christopher Vogle, who wrote for Hollywood movies, also wrote a book called "The Writer's Journey" (1990) based on Campbell's ideas. It is said that this book is now a "must-read" for all Hollywood writers. It seems that folktales have been a powerful force in Hollywood storytelling.

As well as providing universal truths, folktales are an excellent way of learning about the customs, attitudes, and beliefs of other cultures. In both the Chinese folktales in this collection, the main characters perform acts of great kindness for which they are eventually rewarded. In Chinese traditional culture, kindness is a very important value. The stories also tell us a lot about Chinese customs; for example, the gifts that are given on a wedding day or the customs practised hundreds of years ago at the New Year.

The Russian folktale "The Good Peasant's Son" is typical of Russian folktales as it involves a peasant and his good fortune—folktales began among the peasants and in the villages. The Indian folktale "Wisdom for Sale" is the story of how an orphaned Brahman (or Brahmin) boy becomes wealthy and successful. In India the Brahmin class were a class of priests that were powerful in Indian society for many centuries. Even today, Brahmins are the highest of the four Hindu social classes. One message of the story is perhaps that the boy does well because he is a Brahmin. The Guatemalan folktale "Breaking the Chain" tells us a lot about the tradition of magic—particularly evil magic—that exists in Guatemala and in many countries in Central and South America. The Scandinavian folktale "The Golden Apples" provides a good example of earlier beliefs in gods and goddesses. In these stories the gods are much more powerful than human beings but sometimes behave very badly and have many problems of their own.

To last until the present day, a folktale must tell an interesting and entertaining story. The folktales in this collection are all highly entertaining. But they do not only entertain; like all great folktales, they also help us turn the key, enter another world, and experience another time. A folktale may be centuries old, but it can still have meaning for us today.

The Good Peasant's Son

Long ago, in a faraway czardom,⋆ an old peasant lived with his wife and his son, Martin. Time passed and the peasant became very sick. He eventually died, leaving his wife and son alone.

"Oh, my poor husband!" cried his wife. "He was such a good man. How could this happen?"

She cried for days and days. Her son tried to make her feel better, but he couldn't.

Then her sadness changed to worry. At night she looked up into the sky and asked, "What are we going to do? How are we going to live?"

After many weeks like this, she began to take control of herself again and make plans for herself and her poor son.

Her husband had left them some money, 200 roubles. When they had finished almost all the food they had in the house, she gave Martin half the money and told him, "Go into town, my son, and use this money to buy flour, salt, and bread. Hopefully, these supplies will last until the spring. Then we can look for work."

Martin did as his mother asked. He put the money in his pocket and walked into town. As he passed a butcher's store, he saw that a crowd of people had gathered. The butcher had tied an old, sad-eyed hunting dog to a tree. He was beating the dog and the dog was crying with pain.

Martin pushed through the crowd and shouted, "Butcher! Why are you beating this poor dog?"

"Because this 'poor' dog ate some of my best beef this morning! That's why! How can I make a living when this stupid animal eats my best meat?"

⋆czar, czarevna, czardom: the words for a Russian ruler in former times, his daughter, and his country

1

"Oh, but I'm sure he was only hungry. And he looks so sad. Listen. I could use a dog. Why don't I buy him from you? I'll give you 100 roubles for your dog."

The butcher laughed. "You can't be serious! You want to spend 100 roubles on this dog?"

"Yes, I'm serious," replied Martin.

"Then you must be crazy. But you've made me happy even if you are a madman, so give me the 100 roubles and I'll give you the dog."

"Certainly," said Martin and he took the poor, frightened dog away and began to walk back along the road, out of the town, and toward his home.

They walked slowly along until they came to a tree which had fallen by the road. Martin sat down, brought the dog close to him, and looked into his eyes.

"Jourka. That's what I'll name you. And you'll have a safe and happy home with my mother and me."

The grateful dog jumped up and kissed Martin's face with his big pink tongue. He knew that Martin had saved his life and was a kind and gentle person. The two friends then continued walking slowly home, side by side.

When Martin arrived home and told his mother he had spent all their money on an old dog, she was very angry.

"What? You took our money and spent it on this dog? What good can this do us? You know we have nothing. I've made one small cake with the last of the flour we had left. That's our dinner tonight! And there's nothing else! Do you understand? Oh, what would your father do if he could see us now?"

"But mother, this dog is our good luck!" Martin tried to say.

His mother wasn't listening. Without speaking, she gave Martin half of the small cake she had made and left him alone to eat it. Martin shared his small meal with Jourka, the dog.

The next day Martin's mother sent him into town again. But before he left, she sat him down and spoke to him in a serious voice.

"These are our last 100 roubles. You mustn't waste them this time. You must buy supplies so we can eat. Do you hear me?"

"Yes, mother," answered Martin.

He left their house and walked along the road into town, with the 100 roubles in his pocket.

On his way into town Martin passed a small boy who had tied a rope around the neck of an old cat with a bent tail and was dragging her along the road. Martin couldn't bear to see this treatment of a poor animal and asked the boy why he was doing it.

"Because this cat stole one of my mother's special cakes. I'm going to show her what happens to a cat that steals. I'm taking her to the river and I'm going to throw her in!"

"Don't do that," said Martin. "I've been thinking that I would very much like a cat. I'll buy her from you for 100 roubles."

"One hundred roubles! For this old thing with the funny tail! You're joking, aren't you?" laughed the boy.

"Oh no. I'm very serious. And here are the 100 roubles to prove it," said Martin.

The boy couldn't believe it when Martin handed him the money. He happily untied the cat, which jumped into Martin's waiting arms. Martin turned and started walking home with his new friend. He decided to name her Vaska.

When Martin arrived home this time carrying an old cat with a bent tail instead of the food they needed, his mother was very, very angry.

Martin tried to calm her anger. "Mother, this is our second piece of good luck!"

But she threw him out of their house and shouted at him to make his own way in the world and to take the dog and the cat with him.

So Martin left home to look for work and a place to live. His friends, the cat and the dog, never left his side.

One evening, after several days of searching, Martin came into a small village and passed a priest who was just closing the door of his church. The priest was curious about this young man with the dog and the cat, and started a conversation with him to find out more.

"Hello, young man. Where are you going with your two friends?"

"I'm looking for work and a place to live."

"Well, if you work for me for three years, you won't have a contract but you'll have a roof over your head and food for you and your friends. And at the end of that time you'll be paid well."

So Martin accepted the priest's offer and proved to be a good and honest worker.

At the end of the three years the priest came to Martin. "You've been a good worker and now your three years with me have ended. I said that you would be paid well, and you will be. You may choose one of these three payments."

He then put in front of Martin a bag of gold, a bag of silver, and a bag of sand. Martin thought about it. If he chose the gold, he could buy whatever he needed for a long time. He could be almost as wealthy with the silver. But the sand? Why was the priest offering him a bag of sand?

"This must be some kind of test," thought Martin. "And in this simple test I think there is some kind of deeper meaning."

So he stepped forward and said, "I'm going to choose the bag of sand."

"Well, if you don't like silver and gold, of course take the sand," the priest answered, and he handed Martin his bag of sand.

Martin then left the priest to search for more work, taking his bag of sand, Jourka, and Vaska with him. The bag of sand was very heavy and sometimes Martin wanted to leave it behind, but he never did.

After wandering for days he came to a thick, dark forest which was so silent that it seemed no one had ever stepped inside. He eventually came to an open space in the forest. In the center of this area a fire was burning, and a beautiful young woman was tied to a tree in the middle of the fire. The flames were almost touching her and she would soon be burned alive.

When the young woman saw Martin, she cried out, "Oh sir, please put out this fire! I'll bring you good fortune for the rest of your days if you do."

Martin didn't care about the good fortune she promised. He only wanted to help the poor girl, so he quickly took his bag of sand and threw it on the fire to put it out.

"Thank you! Thank you! You've saved my life!" cried the girl as Martin untied her.

When she was free, the girl told Martin that she was the daughter of the czar of the Snake Czardom, and that a cruel czar who was at war with her father had done this to her. She then asked Martin where he had gotten his bag of sand. Martin told her he had chosen the sand, instead of gold and silver, for his three years' work for the priest.

"Well, if you chose that sand, and not silver or gold, it must be very important to you," she said to Martin. "I will always be grateful for your wonderful kindness, and to prove it I want you to have this ring."

As she said this, the girl gave Martin a beautiful gold ring with shining jewels in it.

"This ring is very special," she told him. "It's a magic ring, which will give you anything you desire, even if your desire is to marry a czar's daughter! To unlock its power, just take it off your finger and throw it from one hand to the other. But be careful. You must guard the secret of the ring. If you tell others about its magic, it will bring you great unhappiness."

As soon as she had said this, she turned into a snake and slid quietly away into the forest.

Martin watched her go and then looked down at the ring on his finger. He was suddenly filled with happiness.

He laughed and told Jourka and Vaska, "Do you realize what this means? We don't need to search for work. We'll have everything we need and I can help my poor mother! But let's see this wonderful magic!"

So he took off the ring and threw it from hand to hand, as the girl had told him to do. He then watched in amazement, with Jourka and Vaska, as twelve young men suddenly appeared and said, "Oh master, tell us what in the world you want and we will bring it to you!"

Martin couldn't believe his eyes and ears. He answered, "Good men, take us back to my poor mother!"

And so they returned to his village. His mother, who was filled with guilt and sadness for sending her son away, was very happy to see him again.

"Oh, my son, I've missed you so much and worried so much. Can you ever forgive me?" she cried.

"There's nothing to forgive, dear mother!" cried Martin. "And our life is going to be wonderful now!"

Of course Martin couldn't tell his mother about the magic ring, so he went quietly outside, took the ring off, and threw it from hand to hand. Immediately the twelve young men appeared again and said, "Oh master, tell us what in the world you want and we will bring it to you!"

Martin told them to bring the best food and wine, and the finest meat for Jourka and Vaska. They then celebrated their good fortune.

They all lived together in happiness for many months. Whenever they needed anything, Martin just took off the ring, threw it from hand to hand, and immediately twelve young men appeared, bringing Martin whatever he desired.

◆

Time passed and Martin began to think of marriage. He remembered what the Snake Czar's daughter had told him—that he could have even a czar's daughter! So he asked his mother to go to the czar's palace and ask permission for Martin to marry the czarevna.

His mother was very worried and warned her son that this was a mistake. "The son of a peasant doesn't marry the daughter of a czar. You should look for an ordinary girl to be your wife. You're asking me to do something which is very dangerous. The czar could have our heads cut off for even asking such a thing!"

But Martin had made his decision and wouldn't change his mind, so his mother went to the palace feeling very anxious. When she tried to enter the palace, the guards wouldn't allow her inside. They tried to drag her away but she made such a noise that the czar eventually agreed to see her.

"You must be crazy!" he answered when she asked if Martin could marry his daughter. "How could you imagine that a czar would allow his daughter to marry a peasant!"

"But my son is the kindest and smartest young man in the whole world! He would make any wife proud!" she answered.

"Well, he may be smart. He may be kind. But I'll tell you this. A man who wants to marry the daughter of a czar must send beautiful and expensive gifts. Go away, old woman. Return when you can bring gifts of this kind. Then maybe we'll talk again."

The czar knew that a simple peasant would never be able to provide these beautiful gifts, so he thought this would be the end of the problem.

However, when Martin's mother returned home and told her son, he immediately used the magic ring to produce cloth made of gold, jewels, fine clothes, and many other fine gifts. He then sent his mother back to the palace with these wonderful things.

The riches brought by Martin's mother amazed the czar, but he was also upset, as he did not want his daughter to marry this young man. He repeated that it was impossible for a czar to consider marrying his daughter to a peasant.

"But I've done as you asked!" cried the mother. "You promised me that we would discuss the marriage if I brought these gifts."

The czar didn't know what to do and was quite worried. Then the prime minister spoke.

"My dear Czar. May I make a suggestion?"

"Certainly, Prime Minister!" answered the czar, hoping for a way out of this mess.

"Thank you. If, as this woman says, her son really is the 'smartest young man in all the world,' then he must build a beautiful palace next to yours for his wife to live in. And he must build a bridge of pure silver, with apple trees on either side with fruit of silver and gold. He must also build a great church for the couple's wedding. I suggest that if this woman's son is smart enough to do this, he can marry your daughter. If not, both mother and son should lose their heads."

The czar happily agreed and told Martin's mother that her son must produce these things by the next morning or they would lose their heads.

Martin's mother rushed home with this news, thinking that they would surely die. But Martin wasn't worried. That night he went to the czar's palace, took off his ring, and produced everything that the prime minister had asked for.

The next morning the czar woke up and went outside to greet the day. When he stepped into his garden, he was amazed. There in front of him stood a beautiful, shining palace, a bridge with trees of silver and gold apples, and a great church.

The czar knew then that he had to agree to the marriage, and preparations began in the palace. The czarevna and Martin were dressed in the finest clothes and a beautiful marriage ceremony took place in the great church. For days afterward there were wonderful celebrations at the palace. The young couple then began to live together as man and wife in their palace next to the czar's.

But the czar's daughter wasn't happy. She was silly and proud and very angry that her father had married her to a simple peasant. She wanted to get rid of her husband and tried everything to find out what his secret was, always asking him questions in her sweetest voice.

"You're so smart, my husband. But you're such a mystery too. How are you able to do all these wonderful things? Won't you tell your loving wife?"

But nothing worked. Martin never forgot what the Snake Czar's daughter had told him and he never gave away his secret.

Finally, one night, his wife thought of a new and better idea. She put extra vodka in his cup at dinner and she filled his cup until he was very drunk. She then kept him talking until he finally told her all about the magic ring.

As soon as he was asleep, she took the ring from his finger and used it to take herself, the palace, the bridge, and the church away to a faraway czardom, leaving Martin lying alone in their bed.

When the czar discovered the next morning that his daughter was gone, he was very angry. He demanded to know where she was, but Martin was as shocked and confused as the czar was and couldn't tell him anything. So the czar ordered his guards to build a high stone tower. Martin was locked up in this tower. There was only one tiny window and he was given no food or water. The czar planned to punish him with a long, slow, lonely death.

Jourka, the dog, had been away hunting, and when he returned he was very upset about what had happened to his friend. He ran to Martin's mother's house to tell her and found Vaska the cat lying by the fire sleeping happily.

"What are you doing here?" he shouted at her. "You only think about your own comfort when this terrible thing has happened to our friend, the man who saved our lives! Why aren't you trying to help him when he's in trouble?"

The cat felt very guilty and immediately left the fire. She then listened carefully as Jourka described his plan to trick people in the village out of their food and take it to Martin.

The next day Jourka and Vaska went into the village to carry our their plan. Vaska got under the feet of shoppers as they walked home with their cakes. When they dropped the cakes, Jourka caught them and the dog and the cat ran away.

When little Vaska climbed the stone tower and appeared in the one tiny window with the first cake, Martin cried with joy.

"My dear friends! You haven't forgotten me!"

So their plan was a success and Jourka and Vaska managed to keep Martin alive in this way for a year.

When the year ended, Jourka decided that Martin couldn't live this way for much longer. He told Vaska, "We must go together and try to find the magic ring that has caused all this pain and trouble."

So they left together and crossed mountains, rivers, and even an ocean, with Vaska holding onto Jourka's back.

After many months, they arrived in a faraway czardom and found the beautiful palace that Martin had created for his wife, using the ring. Jourka told Vaska to find her way into the servants' rooms and whenever they needed anything to run quickly and get it for them. Vaska soon became well known in the palace as a good helper, so the servants allowed her and her friend, Jourka, to sleep in the palace. In this way Vaska and Jourka were able to wander around and watch the czarevna closely. They saw that she always wore the ring. They wondered if she took it off to sleep, but her bedroom was the one room that they weren't allowed into, and they were both too big to slide in under the door. Only a mouse was small enough to do this, so they decided to travel to the Czardom of the Mice.

"We must show them that we are strong and powerful so they will be frightened of us and agree to help us," Jourka told Vaska. And this is what they did. They went to the Mouse Czardom and chased and bit the mice until they were so frightened that they surrendered.

"We are powerless against you," the Mouse Czar told them. "What is it that you need? We are your servants."

Jourka told them about the ring, so the Mouse Czar ordered one of the mouse soldiers to slide under the czarevna's door that night and steal the ring. At midnight, when the whole palace was asleep, the mouse soldier went silently into her room and up onto her bed. Then he slipped the ring gently off her finger.

The next morning Jourka and Vaska had the ring back, the ring that would save their friend, so they began to prepare for their long journey home. Vaska put the ring in her mouth and climbed onto Jourka's back. She then used her sharp claws to hold on tight while they started traveling across the ocean again.

After swimming in the rough sea for many days, they were both very tired, but Jourka didn't stop, knowing that the ring would soon be safely back with their dear friend.

Suddenly, Vaska looked up and saw an angry sea bird flying down straight at her. The bird came down and bit Vaska on the head. The pain was so terrible that she couldn't breathe! She watched as the bird flew back up into the sky. But just as Vaska was thinking that her terror was at an end, the bird flew down again, faster this time, and bit her on the head again. Vaska opened her mouth to bite the bird and defend herself, and the ring dropped into the ocean.

"Oh no!" she thought. "How am I going to tell Jourka?"

She waited until they reached land, and as soon as Jourka put her down, she climbed up into a very tall tree.

Jourka looked up, surprised, and asked, "What are you doing up there? Come down!"

"I can't," the cat shouted down to him.

"Why not?" asked Jourka.

"Because you'll kill me!"

"Why? What are you talking about? What do you mean?"

Vaska knew she had to tell him. She also knew he couldn't climb trees. So she stayed up in the tree and explained what had happened to the ring.

"Why didn't you tell me when we were back in the ocean?" Jourka cried.

"Because I can't swim!" cried the frightened cat. "I wanted to wait until I was on dry land to tell you. I knew you'd be angry at me."

"Oh, what are we going to do now," said Jourka as he sat on the sand, his sad eyes looking out to sea.

Then Vaska had an idea. "What about the fish? They know the secrets of the sea. They can help us, can't they?"

"You're right," replied Jourka. "But we must show them our power before they'll help us. Come! Quickly!"

And Jourka swam deep into the ocean to the Fish Czardom. He chased and threatened the fish until they were so frightened that they offered to help him. Jourka explained to the Fish Czar and his fish soldiers about the ring.

Then one shy fish came forward and told them, "Excuse me. I saw a large fish eat something gold earlier today. I don't think it was very good for him because he's now lying dead on the ocean floor."

The Fish Czar immediately ordered his fish soldiers to dive to the bottom of the ocean and search for this fish. They quickly found it and brought it up onto the land. Jourka, who didn't like the taste of fish, watched with excitement as Vaska started eating it. She finally bit into something hard and discovered that it was the ring.

Jourka and Vaska were filled with joy and rushed back to the tower. Vaska then quickly climbed up the stone walls and dropped the ring through the tiny window. Martin, who had not eaten for days, was very happy when he saw it.

"Oh thank you. Thank you, my good, true friends," he cried. "I was almost dead from hunger and thirst!"

He immediately threw the ring from hand to hand and ordered the twelve young men to bring him food and wine. He had his two friends brought up to be with him and celebrate. He then ordered musicians to play music so beautiful that people would be able to do nothing except listen to it and be joyful.

Back in his palace the czar heard the music in the tower. He was very angry that instead of dying Martin seemed to be celebrating! He sent his guards to stop this, but the guards could do nothing except stand and listen to the music. The czar then sent his soldiers to stop this noise, but they could do nothing except stand and sing happily. So in the end, the czar went himself but he found that he couldn't move either. He eventually gave up and told Martin that if he explained everything he would be forgiven.

So Martin went with the czar to the palace and told him the story of the ring and what the czar's daughter had done.

The czar was very sad to hear this and told Martin, "I know that my daughter should be killed for what she has done to you. But she is my daughter. Can you find it in your heart to forgive her?"

Martin was as kind as he had always been. He couldn't have the czarevna killed, so he agreed to take her back. The czar was happy that his daughter would live but he was still sad about her behavior.

13

Martin told him, "Go and rest tonight. And I'm sure everything will look different in the morning."

The czar agreed and went to his room, after ordering his servants to bring Martin his best vodka and to put the finest silk sheets on his bed. That night, while everyone was sleeping, Martin went out into the palace gardens and used the magic ring to bring everything back. The next morning, when the czar went outside, he saw with great happiness the palace, the bridge, and the great church.

Martin and the czarevna lived as man and wife again, and after some time the czarevna realized what a good man Martin really was. She began to love him and they then lived together in happiness. Martin never removed the ring from his finger, and his friends Jourka the dog and Vaska the cat were always by his side.

The Crocodile and the Hunter

A hunter went out into the countryside, far from his village, looking for food. After many hours he was sitting by his fire, eating the meat of the animal he had killed, when he noticed two eyes watching him from the bushes.

The hunter picked up his knife, stood, and asked, "Who are you?"

A wildcat then appeared. "I am Boaji," the cat said. "I can see that your skill has brought you a good day's kill. I'm afraid I haven't had such good luck and I'm very hungry. Could you share your meat with me? If you do, I'll return your kindness in the future."

The hunter shared his meat with Boaji. Boaji ate well and rested for some time by the fire. He then got up, stretched his long, thin body, repeated his promise to the hunter, and walked away into the bushes.

The next day the hunter went out again. He came to a place where the wild grass grew very tall. It was difficult to see where he was going. As he was pushing through the grass, he found a crocodile.

"What are you doing here?" the hunter asked the crocodile. "You should be in the water."

The crocodile told the hunter his story. The night before, he had gone hunting. He had traveled too far from the river and now he couldn't find his way back. He begged the hunter to help him.

"Please show me the way back to the river. If you do this, I'll bring you five loads of fish."

The hunter was happy to help. He tied a rope around the crocodile's foot and led him to the Niger River.

At the water's edge the crocodile thanked him. "I'm very grateful for your kindness. Now, if you untie the rope, I'll go into the river and bring you back five loads of fish as I promised."

The hunter waited high up on the riverbank while the crocodile dived into the dark water.

After a few moments the crocodile rose up out of the water with an enormous fish in his mouth. He swam quickly to the water's edge, came out of the river, moved slowly up the riverbank, and laid the fish in front of the hunter. He then moved slowly back down the riverbank and slid silently into the water.

The hunter inspected the fish and thought, "This will make a fine meal."

Soon the crocodile brought out a second load of fish. These fish were smaller but equally fine-looking. He laid this load lower down the riverbank. The hunter came down and carried the load higher, laying it down next to the big fish.

The crocodile then returned with a third enormous load of fish saying, "Oh dear, this is heavy." This time he left the load at the water's edge. The hunter came down, took hold of the load, and pulled it further up the riverbank.

The crocodile appeared again with a fourth load, saying, "I'm beginning to feel quite tired, but aren't these beauties?" He then laid the load in the shallow water near the riverbank. The hunter came down, picked the fish up out of the water, and carried them high up the riverbank to where the first three loads were.

Finally, after some time, the crocodile returned with the fifth load of fish, which he laid at the edge of the deep water. He called to the hunter, "I'm afraid I have no more energy. I just can't bring these any further. I hope you don't mind."

The hunter came down from the riverbank, walked through the shallow water, and came to the edge of the deep water. He was bending down to pick up the fish when the crocodile suddenly jumped out of the river, closed his enormous jaws around the hunter's foot, and dragged him under the water.

The crocodile raced through the water to his brother crocodiles, who were lying on a small island in the middle of the river. He called to his friends that he had caught a hunter for their dinner and invited them all to come and enjoy the meal. Crocodiles suddenly appeared from every side and crowded round the hunter, moving their heads and tails from side to side and making hungry noises.

"Wait!" shouted the hunter. "I helped your friend! He lost his way and I helped him! And now he's going to eat me! I ask you, is this fair?"

The crocodiles replied, "Let's see if it's fair. You must get four opinions on this question and then we'll decide."

Just then an Asubi, a colored mat, floated down the river. It was old and torn.

The hunter shouted to the Asubi, "Asubi! Please help me!"

"What's wrong?" the mat shouted back.

The hunter told the Asubi what had happened and then asked, "Do you think this is fair?"

The mat replied, "You are a man. I know what men are like. When a mat is new and can be used for many things, they respect it and care for it. They keep it clean and put it away carefully when they have finished using it. But when a mat is old, they forget that it used to be their friend. They throw it away. They throw it into the river. You ask me if life is fair. Life is not fair. You will be fortunate if the crocodile treats you as well as men have treated me!"

The mat floated away down the river.

The crocodile turned to the hunter and asked, "Did you hear that? Did you hear what the Asubi said?"

Then an old, torn piece of cloth came floating down the river.

The hunter cried, "Cloth! Please help me!"

"What's wrong?" the piece of cloth shouted back.

The hunter told the piece of cloth what had happened and then asked, "Do you think this is fair?"

17

The piece of cloth replied, "You are a man. I know what men are like. While a cloth is young, bright, and colorful, they wrap it around their bodies. They believe that the beauty they see in the mirror is their own and not the cloth's. They say, 'Look at me. See how beautiful I am.' But it is the cloth that is beautiful, not them. And the people know this, although they will not admit it, because they fold the cloth up carefully to keep it beautiful when they are not using it. But as soon as the cloth is old, they forget how it used to make them beautiful. They throw it in the river. You ask me if life is fair. Life is not fair. You will be fortunate if the crocodile treats you as well as men have treated me!"

The piece of cloth then floated away down the river.

The crocodile asked, "Did you hear? Did you hear what the cloth said? What do you think now?"

A horse came down to the riverbank to drink. The horse was old and thin. Her owners had forced her to leave their farm because she was too old to work.

The hunter cried, "Horse, please help me!"

"What is the problem?" the horse shouted back.

The hunter told the horse what had happened and then asked, "Tell me. Do you think this is fair?"

The horse replied, "You are a man. I know what men are like. When a horse is young, they look after her well. She has a warm home. The boys brush her and give her the best grass. She is given as much food as she can eat. But when the horse is old and cannot work or have babies, when she is weak and sick, they take her out into the countryside and say, 'Look after yourself now.' You ask me if life is fair. Life is not fair. Look at me! You will be fortunate if the crocodile treats you as well as men have treated me!"

The horse then walked slowly away.

The crocodile said to the hunter, "You heard what the old horse said, didn't you? You've had three opinions now."

Then a wildcat came down to the riverbank, looking for fish. It was Boaji.

The hunter cried, "Boaji, please help me!"

"What's wrong?" asked Boaji.

The hunter told Boaji what had happened and asked him if this was fair. Boaji thought for a moment and replied, "That is difficult to judge. First, I must know all the facts. I want to hear the crocodile's side of the story too. But if I do this, the crocodile must accept my final decision.

"Of course," the crocodile replied.

Boaji asked the crocodile, "How did the hunter bring you here?"

"He tied a rope around my foot and dragged me here," answered the crocodile.

Boaji asked, "Did it hurt?"

The hunter interrupted, "That's not true! He's lying! I didn't *drag* him!"

Boaji stopped the hunter. "I cannot judge that until I have seen it. Come here and show me exactly what you did."

So the crocodile and the hunter came out of the river and onto the shore. Boaji told the hunter to tie the rope around the crocodile's foot exactly as he had done before. The hunter did this.

Boaji then asked the crocodile, "Is this what it was like?"

"Oh yes," answered the crocodile. "This is what it was like. And soon it began to hurt."

Boaji said, "I can't decide that yet. The hunter is going to have to lead you back again so I can examine this accurately. Do as I say and I will follow you."

The hunter picked up the rope and led the crocodile back into the tall grass, while Boaji followed. They walked for some time in the hot sun until eventually they came to the place where the hunter had met the crocodile.

"This is the place," said the hunter.

Boaji asked the crocodile, "Was it here?"

"Yes, it was here. And from here the hunter dragged me behind him to the river."

Boaji asked, "And you were not satisfied?"

The crocodile answered, "No, I wasn't."

Boaji told the crocodile, "Good. You punished the hunter for hurting you by dragging him into the river. So now this argument is finished. To avoid more quarrels of this kind, the hunter must untie the rope and leave you here in the tall grass. This is my decision."

"What!" shouted the crocodile angrily. He brought his tail down hard against the earth and spun around to face Boaji and the hunter. "I'll never find my way back to the river!"

The hunter looked at Boaji and smiled. They then left the crocodile there screaming in anger. The hunter thanked Boaji as they walked away.

The time comes when everyone is treated as he has treated others.

Breaking the Chain

Juanantes Dios Rodrigues was a poor farmer. He was a good man, a good husband. He worked hard and lived a simple life.

One night Juanantes took a bottle of whiskey to the field behind his house. He didn't usually drink alcohol. He hated the taste, although people said it was better than most other pleasures in life. Some people had even found the "good light" after drinking alcohol. A person who experienced the "good light" was able to leave this earth and, for a short time, stay between two worlds, in a place where death couldn't touch them. This light meant good health, long life, happiness, good business. Everyone searched for this light. But Juanantes didn't drink—until that night.

There was no reason for his drinking—nothing to celebrate, no anger to drown, or sadness to forget. But he couldn't fight his desire on that night. When he had finished the bottle, he heard a voice. The voice commanded him to go to the top of a mountain called the Hill of Sand on the first Tuesday of the ninth month, at midnight. There he would find a large fire in the forest. He would see a bag by the fire. He had to approach the fire and pick up the bag before the fire burned it. Inside the bag there would be treasure and something else, a mandate. He had to do exactly what the mandate ordered him to do.

On the first Tuesday of the ninth month his wife, Cardenala, went with him to the Hill of Sand. They left at midnight, as the voice had instructed, and walked through the forest. They were afraid but excited at the same time. The noises of the night were all around them. Eyes shone in the dark, watching them.

Juanantes had told Cardenala about the voice during a moment of weakness, as he lay there recovering from his night of drinking. He knew now, as she pushed him forward in the darkness, that it had been a mistake to tell Cardenala. Since he had told her about the voice, he had had no peace. He couldn't work. His farm and his animals had suffered. Cardenala wouldn't leave him alone, day or night. Even in silence they knew each other's thoughts.

To him the mysterious voice he had heard was like an evil curse. But not to Cardenala. To her it was a way of escaping from their poverty, the way to the "good light."

Juanantes wanted the treasure but at the same time he feared it. He wasn't sure he should do what the voice had commanded. But Cardenala's desire infected him. She decided for both of them. They would go to the Hill of Sand. They would do exactly what the voice had told them to do. They would find the treasure. She planned. She worried. If the bag contained money, how would they spend it? If it contained jewels, who could they sell them to? She woke him up with her fears.

"The police might ask questions. If there's gold in the bag, what will we do?"

The more she pushed, the more full of doubt he became.

"I may be poor, but at least I'm happy," he told her.

She called him a coward and threatened to go alone. So they went together on that dark night.

At one point Cardenala wanted to turn back. She suddenly had a black thought. She could see danger waiting for them. She called to Juanantes, but it was too late. He didn't hear her. He didn't answer. He didn't even turn his head. There was no moon. Cardenala could only see his white hat in the darkness.

He walked on without stopping, without thinking. He wasn't cautious or indecisive now. There was another Juanantes inside his skin, fingers holding tightly onto his machete, eyes staring. What had caused this change in him? What was driving him forward?

At last they came to the fire, an enormous, blinding fire. Juanantes waited for a moment, silent, thinking. Should they turn around? Could they escape this? Forget it had ever happened? Cardenala said nothing. Then Juanantes rushed forward and saw, where the voice had told him it would be, an old cloth bag. He quickly took the bag, almost burning his face in the flames, and returned to Cardenala. Suddenly ambitious again and filled with curiosity about what was in the bag, he took Cardenala's hand and they ran from the place.

They could see nothing in the darkness. They felt the outside of the bag. Bones? And something heavier, with a weight like metal. Juanantes opened it and felt inside. It was impossible to see but yes, there were the bones of a man, a machete, and in a smaller bag, a bottle of whiskey and some gold coins. Was this the treasure of the dead? It was all a mystery. He found a metal box and opened it. Inside he could feel some kind of paper—a document. This must be the mandate.

The events of later that night have never been fully understood. In the early hours, when it was still dark, as Cardenala lay sleeping in their bedroom, Juanantes opened the metal box and read the mandate. The mandate told him to kill a man, Prudencio Salvatierra. Kill? Juanantes shook with fear.

He left quietly and went to a bar to have a drink. He needed a drink now, to calm himself. He needed to think. He was lifting his glass to his mouth when he heard someone say the name of Prudencio Salvatierra. The sound of that name filled him with hatred. His glass crashed to the floor. He couldn't see. He couldn't think. He wanted this man's blood. He had to *spill* this man's blood! He pulled out his machete and rushed toward Prudencio Salvatierra.

"Fight or be killed like a dog!" he shouted.

Prudencio pulled out his machete. "Who are you? What do you want with me?"

Juanantes attacked him. There were screams. People were running. Tables and chairs were knocked over as people crowded around to watch. Juanantes was wild, with the strength of ten men. His machete came down again and again on Prudencio

Salvatierra until the bar was red with his blood. Prudencio had no chance. Within minutes he lay dead, his body in pieces.

Later, Juanantes was questioned again and again by the judge. Why had he fought with Prudencio Salvatierra? Juanantes could give no answer. There was no logic. No, they had never met before. No, he was not an enemy—until that night. Until the moment when Juanantes heard his name, the name he recognized, the name that was written in the mandate.

Juanantes was found guilty of murder and sent to prison for ten years.

Cardenala found employment as a servant near the prison, so that she could visit Juanantes every Sunday. After many Sundays they began to talk of when Juanantes would be freed.

"What are you going to do?" asked Cardenala.

Juanantes heard her words again and again in his mind. What are *you* going to do? What are *you* . . . ? Not *we*. He looked hard at Cardenala, as a policeman looks at a suspect, searching for signs. Was she planning to stay in the city? Was there another man?

"Tell me, Cardenala. Aren't you coming back with me?"

"No."

Her quiet answer, her guilt, hit him. For a moment he couldn't speak.

"All right. All right. But I must go back to our village. You know that, don't you?"

"Yes, I know. But I don't care what you say. I'm not going with you. I went to see the priest. He told me it was the work of the devil. I'm not going to fall into that trap again."

"The priest? Why did you go to the priest?" he asked her.

"My boss wanted me to. He was worried about me. He's very kind to me."

Juanantes knew it then. He knew that he was losing Cardenala. Prison was bad, like a kind of death. Four walls. Always the same four walls. The desperate faces. The waiting. The long, lonely nights. But losing Cardenala? No. Impossible. There

24

was nothing he could do, though. When the evil light has fallen on a man, everything goes wrong. He would have to go back to their village alone.

The following Sunday Cardenala came to visit as usual.

"You've come," he said.

"Of course I've come. What do you mean?"

"Well, I thought . . ."

"You thought! You thought! You think too much!" laughed Cardenala.

In her mouth a new gold tooth shone.

"And this tooth?" asked Juanantes.

"Oh, my boss paid for it."

"Your boss again. And you paid him back?"

"Of course. Stop questioning me!"

Juanantes asked again. "Are you coming back with me?"

"No, Juanantes."

Short and sharp. It cut his heart.

"Well, at least . . ." He stopped. His voice left him. "At least this way I know," he finally managed to say. "These things happen to people who have swallowed the evil light."

His sad eyes grew hard as he watched Cardenala's face.

On his last day he gathered his few remaining possessions—a few clothes, old and full of holes now, and the torn pieces of a picture of Cardenala. He had torn the picture up, put it back together, torn it up, so many times. But still he saved the pieces.

He went to a hotel to stay that night and filled in the form at reception with his full name, Juanantes Dios Rodriguez. Then he left with no explanation. Why? The keys! Those large, heavy room keys reminded him of his prison cell, of hundreds of cells. He wandered around without sleeping or eating until his stomach ached with hunger. But he couldn't sit in the café, where people stood in line like prisoners. So he walked along the dusty road toward the mountains. He knew something still had to be done.

He had killed Prudencio Salvatierra ten long years ago. Now he had to obey the mandate's final order.

He went to where he had been living with Cardenala. Nothing had changed. Everything was as it had always been. The trees, the rocks. It even seemed that the same old dogs still, now, after ten years, slept in the sun.

Juanantes felt full of sorrow. But he wasn't *doing* anything. He wasn't living. And so, without further thought, he called on the wise old man, Tata Guamarachito, for help.

"It's no good being in this condition," the old man told Juanantes. "You're good for nothing. Nothing goes right. I know why you're suffering. As a young man the same thing happened to me. Yes, I can help you. I can help you understand what you're dealing with. I can advise you about what you have to do."

"But I don't want to do what the mandate ordered!" shouted Juanantes. "I have no enemies."

"It's not necessary to have an enemy."

"Yes, but to bury the evil light, this evil light, which by accident or pure bad luck I've fallen into, I know that I have to write a mandate, an order to kill someone. I have to put that into the metal box. But I keep telling you: I have no one to kill! It's hopeless anyway. The evil light has entered my body, like sand. I cough. I even cough blood! It's in me. It got into me in prison. I . . . "

As he was speaking he lost control and fell, coughing, to the ground.

But the old man was still not persuaded. "How do you know it's the evil light?" he asked calmly.

Juanantes told him that pieces of the evil light were everywhere. He saw them clearly, dancing around him, causing him to cough, giving him night fevers.

"Then get away from them," was the old man's advice.

But Juanantes asked again, with anger now, "How can I do this if I have no enemies?"

"Calm down. I'm only trying to help. And don't blame yourself so much. You've paid your debt in prison for killing Salvatierra. You killed fairly. The two of you faced each other as men, with machetes. Salvatierra died and you lived. If you hadn't followed the mandate to kill someone, you would have been killed yourself. Because it was written."

But Juanantes was still unhappy. "It would be better if I were dead."

"Don't talk like that. In my experience it's never better to be dead than alive."

"What has to be done then? What must I do?"

"You must light the fire of evil light and write your own mandate to put into the metal box by the fire."

"But I've told you. I can't write this mandate."

"Juanantes, if you let me, I'll show you a way to break the chain of death, the chain which has caught you."

"No, Tata. If I break the chain of death, it will only bring me more tragedy. More sorrow! I . . ."

The old man interrupted. "The evil light that's around you is responsible for many deaths. It's time to put an end to it. I've told you that I can show you how to break this chain. Be brave. Believe in me. Write your own mandate. Use your own words. The words of Juanantes Dios Rodriguez, a man of honor. Then we'll do together what has to be done."

They arranged to meet in nine weeks, when the night would be at its blackest. On that night they waited, hidden behind some trees. They heard the sound of a horse coming, slowly, cautiously. Juanantes lit the fire. The horse and rider slowly approached the fire. The rider got down, with his gun in his hand. A moment passed. There was silence. Then the rider rushed toward the fire, took the bag which Tata Guamarachito and Juanantes had left there, jumped onto his horse, and rode away into the night.

"See how simple it was," said Tata Guamarachito, throwing his arm around Juanantes's shoulder. "Look at you! Already the evil

27

light is leaving you. The sadness is lifting. But have you broken the chain of death? The bones, your machete—the same machete you used to kill Salvatierra—the bottle of whiskey, the gold, were all there in the bag. But you didn't order anyone to be killed. So what did you order instead? What did you write on that piece of paper, with your signature, which you put in the metal box?"

"That one thing I can't tell you. It's my secret."

"But you didn't order anyone to be killed?"

"No. I told you, I couldn't. I have no enemies."

"Then what was your order?"

"I repeat, Tata, that's my secret."

"All right. I respect that."

"Please forgive me, Tata."

"There's no need. Men with secrets are always interesting to me. But let me tell you. You're breaking a chain, a chain that has caused many deaths and destroyed many lives. I'm . . ." Tata Guamarachito coughed, the heavy cough of a smoker. "I'm close to 100 years old. But when I was your age . . . How old are you? About thirty? When I was your age, I fell into the evil light. I was ordered to kill a man, Belisario Consuegra, a man I had never met. A man I had never seen. But one day, I was at a market buying a horse and I heard someone shouting, 'Belisario! Belisario Consuegra!' My blood turned cold. I couldn't see or hear. I took out my machete, found him, and ordered him to defend himself or be killed like an animal. He fought. But I killed him. I cut him into pieces. The smell of his blood made me crazy."

"But did you bury your evil light with a mandate?"

"Yes, Juanantes. There was a man, a Mexican, my enemy. My mandate was found by Placido Salgaespera, and Salgaespera killed the Mexican with his machete. Salgaespera's mandate was then found by Remigio Huertas, who killed Salgaespera's enemy, and it has continued in this way. Say that you've broken the chain, Juanantes. Tell me this."

28

But Juanantes only sat silently watching the sunrise. He always watched the sunrise, but had never liked the morning. Now, however, freed from the evil light, it seemed to be the most beautiful dawn he could ever experience. Suddenly he wanted Cardenala. He wanted her so badly. But he stopped these thoughts as soon as they began. Why should he want her? He knew now that Cardenala was part of the evil light which had brought him to this place. Because of her, Prudencio Salvatierra now lay cold in the ground.

When the sun had fully risen, he offered Tata Guamarachito payment for his services. The old man wouldn't accept money.

"I want only to know your secret. The mandate that the horseman read."

But without speaking, Juanantes walked away.

He was going down the mountain when he suddenly changed his mind, turned, and started back toward Tata Guamarachito. Walking, then running, shouting, "Tata! Wait! I will! I will share my secret with you!"

When he reached the place where they had sat, he bent down and whispered in the old man's ear.

"Is that true? Was that really your mandate?" asked the old man, smiling, trying to hold back his tears of joy.

"Yes. Yes. That she too would be torn up when the picture was torn up. Now I know, Tata, that when I tore up Cardenala's picture in prison it began to free me, to free me from her evil power. Woman, when she goes bad, is the worst of all evil lights. Because of this, my mandate ordered the unknown rider to take the picture of the first person with an untrue heart that he found, the first unfaithful friend or lover, and tear it into pieces. There are many ways of destroying someone."

Lukas's Luck

Lukas had been a very wealthy farmer, but he hadn't managed his farm wisely and had been very careless with his money. He realized too late what a fool he had been, when he lost everything. Now he and his wife lived in poverty in a tiny house, which could hardly be called a house. The cracks in the walls made it impossible to keep warm. Rain came in through the holes in the roof. Their life was a constant struggle.

They had always prayed for a child, but during their years of wealth God had never listened. Now they were poor and had nothing and his wife gave birth to a baby daughter.

"Oh, what are we going to do?" his wife cried. "We don't have food for ourselves. How are we going to take care of this poor little stranger?"

"We'll find a way," Lukas said. "She's a gift from God, so he'll help us find a way. But first we must have her christened. We must ask someone to be our daughter's godmother."

They had no relatives in the area, so Lukas went to ask their neighbor's wife.

"My husband and I are only poor peasants, like you. Why should we add your child to our list of money worries?" was her answer.

Lukas returned home with the bad news.

"What can you expect?" asked his wife sadly. "When we were rich, everyone wanted to know us and be our friends. Even the mayor invited us to his home. But now we have nothing and not even a poor peasant woman will help us."

She was very worried about their little baby. Winter was almost at its end, but it was still very cold. At night the earth froze and in the morning the houses and trees were covered in snow. They had no clothes for their child, only old bits of cloth. And her bed was the cold, hard ground.

Lukas's wife kissed their baby and cried, "My poor darling. My poor little darling."

Then suddenly a happy thought came to her. She told Lukas to go and ask the mayor's wife to be their child's godmother. She was godmother to the mayor's child and was certain that the mayor's wife would do the same for them. Lukas didn't feel so certain, but he went to ask her.

With a heavy heart, Lukas walked past the fields and farm buildings that used to be his. He arrived at the mayor's house and gave his wife's good wishes to the mayor's wife. He then asked if she would be godmother to their child.

"You know how hard things are at the moment," she answered. "Everyone's struggling. I can't afford to help someone as poor as you. Why are you asking me, anyway? Isn't there someone else you could ask?"

"Well, my wife is godmother to your child," he answered simply.

"Oh! I see! So this is a debt that I have to repay, is it?" was her angry reply. "Is that the only reason your wife agreed to be our child's godmother? And tell me, what help is your wife to our child now, when you have nothing! How dare you come to my home and insult me like this! I wouldn't be your child's godmother if you paid me in gold!"

Lukas left in tears. When he got home, he described what had happened at the mayor's house. His wife was desperately unhappy, but he told her not to be discouraged. He was going to take their child to the christening himself and ask the first person he met on the road to be her godmother.

His wife, crying, wrapped their child in an old blanket to protect her from the winter winds and put her in her father's arms. Lukas dressed as warmly as he could and started on his journey. He carried his baby sadly but proudly along the road.

After several hours he saw an old woman, dressed in old, torn, dirty clothes, walking very slowly on her old, bent legs. He hesitated for a moment and then walked up to her, explained their situation, and asked her if she would be godmother to their baby.

The old woman smiled warmly, took the tiny baby in her arms and said, "Yes, of course I will. It will be an honor to be godmother to such a sweet little baby, whose father loves her so much."

They continued together to the church.

The priest was just getting ready to leave when his assistant hurried up to him and whispered that some people were arriving.

"Oh no!" said the priest, who wanted to get home for his supper. "Who is it and what do they want at this late hour?"

"It's only Lukas," answered his assistant. "You know—the one who lost everything. He's as poor as the poorest peasant now."

As they approached the church, the godmother saw that the assistant was whispering something unkind to the priest. So, as they entered, she pulled from her old dress a golden ducat★ and pressed it into the priest's hand. The priest was amazed. He looked at the ducat, then at the old woman in her torn clothes. He then quickly whispered to his assistant to prepare for the baby's christening.

The christening ceremony that followed was suitable for the wealthiest of merchants. The little girl received the name Marishka. After the christening, the priest walked with them to the door of the church. His assistant walked with them all the way to the gate, hoping for a nice reward. The old woman gave him a golden ducat, which he received gratefully.

When Lukas and the old woman reached the place where they had first met, she handed the baby to him. She then reached into her pocket and pulled out another golden ducat, which she put inside the baby's blanket.

★ducat: an old coin used in the former Czechoslovakia

She smiled at Lukas and said, "This is my gift to your child. This will provide enough money to bring her up well and give her everything she needs. This child will bring you and your wife great joy and comfort, and when she grows into a woman she will have a long and happy marriage."

The kind godmother then touched the ground and suddenly a beautiful rose bush appeared, covered in sweet-smelling flowers.

Lukas bent down to admire the lovely flowers and then turned to thank the old woman. But she was gone! He was amazed and confused.

"Goodbye!" he called. "Thank you, kind godmother!"

He stood there, holding little Marishka, looking all around him. He would probably have stood there for hours if Marishka hadn't started crying for her supper.

So he began walking, and as he walked he thought about all the wonderful things that had happened to him that day. At one point he stopped and felt in Marishka's blanket, to make sure that the ducat was still there, that he hadn't dreamed it. He took it out and suddenly it became ten ducats and fell out of his hand all over the ground. Again, he stood there, not speaking, full of amazement. He gathered the ducats up, laughing, put them in his pockets, and almost ran with Marishka back to his home.

Lukas's wife had been waiting anxiously at home, hungry, thirsty, and cold. There was no food in the house and no money. She was very surprised when Lukas ran in with a happy smile on his face and told her all about the kind godmother.

When he finished, he told his wife to take the godmother's christening gift out of Marishka's blanket. The wife reached in and pulled out the ducat. Suddenly there were ten, twenty, thirty ducats! She cried out in happiness and surprise. The ducats flew out of her hands and rolled all over the floor. They both began to pick the ducats up, but wherever there was one, another ten appeared! In the end there was a beautiful golden pile shining in front of them. They fell onto the floor, laughing and crying at the same time.

Then Lukas's wife was suddenly full of fear. "Could this money be an evil curse? Maybe the woman is an evil spirit who wants to buy our souls?"

Lukas laughed. "Don't be silly," he told her. "What evil spirit would go into a church?"

But Lukas knew this godmother wasn't an ordinary woman. Maybe she was a good spirit sent by God to help them. He warned his wife, however, that they must guard their secret. He told her to hide the money and not tell anyone the true story.

He then took one ducat for the mayor to change, so he could buy eggs, flour, bread, and milk.

When he asked his wife what else he should buy, she immediately answered, "Our land, our house, our animals, our fields!"

"Tomorrow morning!" Lukas replied happily.

Then his wife became very serious and said, "But Lukas, please manage them more carefully this time."

Lukas took her in his arms and told her quietly, "I promise to do this, for you and our child. I've been very silly and caused us much unhappiness and worry. But I've learned my lesson. Please believe me."

He then left to get their supplies. While he was out, his wife sat holding her baby and dreaming happily about their future.

After some time Lukas returned with the mayor's servant, who was carrying buckets of fresh milk, a basket of eggs, and some wonderful cakes.

"The mayor's wife sends her good wishes to you both and has sent me to help you in any way I can," the servant told her.

Lukas's wife thanked her and watched as the servant then began preparing a fine soup for them on the fire. Lukas had also bought three soft feather beds, which he put by the fire.

The next day Lukas went to buy back their farm. The mayor's wife was extremely curious to know how Lukas and his wife had become wealthy again since his visit to their house the day before. So while Lukas was out, she visited his wife and asked questions. But Lukas's wife didn't give away their secret. She just told her that Marishka's godmother had very kindly given them enough money to help them start again.

After the mayor's wife left, Lukas's wife sat by the fire, thinking about their kind godmother. She thanked her for giving them a second chance in life.

Lukas did buy back all their property and this time he managed it wisely. He built handsome, solid farm buildings and a beautiful house for his family. He bought the very best animals and in the fall his fields were full of healthy golden wheat and corn. His farm became the best in the region. Lukas and his wife were loved and admired, as they were good neighbors, generous and helpful to any poor farmer who was having bad luck.

Marishka was a wonderful child. She gave Lukas and his wife great joy and comfort, as her godmother had said she would. When she became a woman her beauty attracted a wealthy prince, who asked her to be his wife. She married him and lived a long and happy life. Lukas and his wife grew old in good health. In the evenings they often sat by the fire and talked about the time when the kind godmother appeared and changed Lukas's luck.

Wisdom for Sale

A poor Brahman* boy lost his parents in a terrible flood. He was left alone, an orphan with no home and no job. He didn't know what he would do or how he would live. But he was a very smart boy and had learned many things from his father, so it didn't take him long to think of a great idea. One day he walked into town, hired the smallest, cheapest place he could find in the marketplace, and opened a store. He spent the little money he had on paper, ink, and a pen. Over his store he put a sign saying "Wisdom for sale."

All around him in the busy marketplace merchants owned large, attractive stores selling things that people needed, like cloth, meat, fruit, and vegetables. The Brahman boy stood outside his little store all day, calling out, "Wisdom for sale! Good prices! Wisdom of all kinds! Wisdom!"

People passing his store, who had come to buy supplies for their homes and families, thought he was odd but amusing too. Instead of buying his wisdom they crowded around, laughing at him and shouting.

"If you're so wise, boy, why do you have such a tiny store and why do you wear such old, dirty clothes?"

"Oh wise one, can you make my wife stop telling me what to do?"

But the boy was patient.

One day a merchant's son was walking through the marketplace and heard the boy shouting, "Wisdom! Get it here! Good prices!" He followed the boy's voice through the colorful, noisy crowds until he came to his tiny store. This merchant's son was very rich, but also very stupid. He didn't understand what

*Brahman: the highest social level of followers of the Hindu religion

the boy was selling. He thought it was something he could eat or hold. He asked the Brahman boy the price per kilo.

The Brahman boy answered, "I don't sell wisdom by weight. I sell it by quality."

So the merchant's son put down a rupee and said, "All right. I'd like a rupee's worth of wisdom, please."

The boy's face suddenly became very serious. He put the rupee in his pocket and told the merchant's son to sit down. Then he also sat down. He looked carefully at the merchant's son's face for a moment, then up at the sky. Then he took out a piece of paper, closed his eyes, took a deep breath, opened his eyes, and wrote. When he had finished, he folded the paper, waved his hand over it three times, stood up, and gave it to the merchant's son. On the paper were the words, "It is not wise to stand and watch two people fighting."

The boy told him in a serious voice, "Keep this with you always."

The merchant's son was very excited. He quickly went home and ran into the house, shouting, "Father, you won't believe what happened to me today. Come quick and see what I've bought!"

When his father read the paper, he couldn't believe his eyes. He screamed at his son, "You stupid boy! I can't believe my son paid a rupee for this nonsense! Everyone knows you shouldn't stand and watch two people fighting! Who sold you this garbage?"

His son then told him about the boy and his little store.

The father immediately went to the store.

"Aha! There you are!" he shouted, when he entered the tiny store and saw the Brahman boy.

"Yes, here I am," replied the boy. "And who are you?"

"I'm the father of the fool who bought this piece of nonsense from you!" He threw the piece of paper at the boy. "You're a thief and you've cheated my son! Yes, he's a fool, but you're a thief! Return the rupee he paid you or I'll call the police!"

The Brahman boy read the paper and said, "If you don't like my goods, you can return them. Give me back my goods and I'll return your money."

"I've just returned your goods. Now give me my son's rupee or I'll call the police!"

"Sir, you have not returned my goods. You've only returned the piece of paper. If you want your money, you must return my wisdom. You must sign a document saying that your son will never use my advice, that he will always stand and watch two people fighting."

"What? You must be joking!" shouted the angry merchant.

But by now a crowd had gathered around to watch the argument and they agreed with the boy.

"He's right, you know. The man's only returned the paper."

"Yes, who do you think you are? Trying to frighten a poor storekeeper!"

So the father agreed to sign the document and the Brahman boy then returned his money. The merchant was secretly thankful that it had been so easy to get his silly son out of this mess.

The king of this region had two queens. These two queens were extremely jealous of each other and they argued about everything. Their maids supported them, of course, and argued as bitterly as their queens. One day each queen sent her servant to the marketplace. By chance both maids went to the same store at the same time and, unfortunately, wanted to buy the same melon. An argument developed.

"Excuse me, but I was just going to buy that melon."

"Oh, what a pity. I got it first."

"Yes, but you got it first because you pushed in front of me."

"Excuse me, I didn't push in front of you."

"You did! My hand was just reaching out to pick it up and you pushed in front."

"I didn't!"

"You did!"

"I didn't!"

"You did!"

"Did not!"

"Did!"

"Did not!"

They began to argue so loudly that the store owner ran away in fear. The two girls fell out of the store onto the ground, pulling each other's hair and hitting each other.

The merchant's son was passing, heard the maids fighting, and stopped to watch them, as his father had instructed him to. One of the maids noticed the merchant's son and ordered him to be her witness.

"You saw that! She hit me!"

The other maid interrupted. "No, she hit me! You saw her, didn't you! You're *my* witness."

They continued fighting until suddenly one of them said, "Oh dear! Look at the time. My queen's expecting me."

They both immediately picked themselves up, shook the dirt from their dresses, gathered their shopping, and hurried back to the palace.

When the two maids returned to the palace, they told their queens all about the argument. The queens were naturally very angry and complained to the king. The maids had also told their queens about the witness who had seen everything. Each queen ordered the merchant's son to be her maid's witness or have his head cut off. The king sent a messenger to the merchant's house with his queens' commands.

The merchant and his son were very worried when they received these commands.

"We need to see the Brahman boy immediately and ask him what to do," said the father.

They rushed to the little store and told the Brahman boy the whole story. He thought for a moment and said, "This is a difficult situation. I can help you, but it will cost 500 rupees."

The merchant happily paid this. The boy's face became very serious. He took a deep breath, closed his eyes for a moment, opened his eyes, and said, "When they call you to the palace, pretend to be crazy. Pretend that you don't understand anything."

The next day the king called the merchant's son to the palace as a witness. The boy behaved as the Brahman boy had instructed him to. Eventually the king lost patience with this madman and ordered him out of the palace. The merchant's son was delighted with this success and told everyone about the Brahman boy's great wisdom. The Brahman boy was soon well-respected in the marketplace.

But the merchant wasn't happy. His son would now have to pretend to be crazy for the rest of his life or the king would find out and cut off his head. So the merchant and his son went back to the Brahman boy for more wisdom. For another 500 rupees the Brahman boy advised them to go back to the king at a carefully chosen time and tell him the whole story.

He told them, "If you approach him at the right time, when he's relaxed and in a good mood, he'll think it's funny and forgive you. But choose your time well. Make sure he's in a good mood."

The merchant's son followed his advice. He went to the palace on a beautiful warm evening as the sun was setting. He felt that no one could be in a bad mood on a beautiful evening like this. It was after dinner and he knew the king had eaten well because kings always eat well. The guards presented him to the king. He was right. The king was in a very good mood.

The merchant's son told him the whole story and begged for the king's forgiveness for doing such a silly thing. The king thought the story was very funny and forgave him. He told him not to worry as everyone makes mistakes sometimes.

When the merchant's son had left the palace, the king sat alone, thinking about the story. He was very curious about this Brahman boy and his special talent. So he sent for the boy and asked him if he had any more wisdom to sell.

The Brahman boy said, "Of course. I have plenty to sell, especially to a king. But my wisdom isn't cheap. It will cost you 100,000 rupees.

The king didn't hesitate. He paid him 100,000 rupees and the Brahman boy followed his usual routine. He sat, he thought, he looked carefully at the king's face, and then at the sky above. Then he took a deep breath, closed his eyes, opened them again, and wrote on a piece of the king's special paper. When he had finished writing, he folded the piece of paper, waved his hand over it three times, and gave it to the king. On the piece of paper the king read the words, "Think deeply before you do anything." The king thought this advice was very wise and he had it written in gold letters on all his royal plates and cups and sewn on his fine pillows and sheets so he would never forget it.

Some months later the king became very sick. He didn't realize that one of his queens and his minister were planning his murder. As part of their plan, they had paid the king's doctor to put poison into his medicine. One night, when the king was taking his medicine, he lifted his golden cup up to his lips and, just before he started to drink, he noticed the words he had had written on the cup, "Think deeply before you do anything." Without suspecting anything, the king thought about the words, lowered his cup, and looked at the medicine in it.

The doctor, who was standing there watching this, became very nervous. He was full of guilt and fear, certain that the king had guessed that his medicine was poisoned.

While the king was lying there thinking, the doctor suddenly threw himself at his feet and cried, "Forgive me, my king!"

Before the king could say anything, the doctor told him what the queen and the minister were planning and how they had involved him. He then began to cry and begged again to be forgiven.

The king was completely shocked at first, but as soon as he had recovered, he called his guards and had the doctor locked up. He then sent for his minister and his wife. When the guards brought them into his room, the king told them what had just happened and that he had put the doctor in prison.

His wife immediately said, "Oh, I'm so pleased! I always knew that man was crazy but this wild story he's invented is proof!"

"Crazy, you say? Wild story, you say?" answered the king. "Let's see who's telling the truth. Drink my medicine."

The queen immediately fell at the king's feet, admitted her guilt, and begged for his forgiveness. The minister just stood there silently, looking very depressed. The king ordered his guards to take them both away and cut off their heads.

The Brahman boy was then sent for by the king. When the guards brought the boy into his room, the king thanked him for saving his life. He made the boy his new minister and arranged for him to live in the palace. A fine apartment and beautiful clothes were prepared for him. The boy lived happily in the palace as a wealthy man of honor and remained the king's most trusted adviser for the rest of his life.

The Wooden Horse

Many centuries ago there was a great and powerful king of Persia named Sabur. He was a kind and generous king, who helped the poor and showed respect to everybody. On public holidays King Sabur always opened his palace to the people of his city. The people celebrated for days and brought the king and his family beautiful gifts.

On one holiday a wizard came to the palace to give the king his new invention. The wizard was a smart inventor, who knew all about magic and the mysteries of the world and could make unusual things. The king loved anything scientific and technical and he asked the wizard to show him his invention.

So the wizard presented him with a horse, which was made of beautiful wood as black as the night. Its shining eyes were pure gold and it had jewels in its fine head. It was a very suitable gift for a king. The king admired the horse's beauty and asked the wizard what it could do.

"My Lord," the wizard answered, "if you get on this horse, it will carry you wherever you want to go. It can ride through the sky and race through one year in a single day."

The king thought this invention was very special and he said to the wizard, "Show me how this horse of yours works. By Allah, if you're telling the truth, I'll give you whatever your heart desires."

So the wizard climbed onto the horse's back, pressed its stomach, and the horse suddenly flew up into the sky and around in circles above the palace. Everyone was amazed as they watched this.

"So now, wizard, you may ask for anything and I'll give you whatever you desire."

This wizard had heard that the king had three beautiful daughters and that the youngest was especially beautiful. People

43

often talked of her beauty and said that she was like the sun and the moon. So the wizard asked the king to give him his youngest daughter as his wife. The king immediately agreed and commanded a servant to bring his daughter. But the three daughters had been watching and listening from behind a curtain. The youngest saw that her husband was at least 100 years old and very ugly. She couldn't believe that her father would marry her to this horrible old man with a face like a monkey's. She ran to her room, fell onto her bed, and cried.

Her brother, Prince Kamar Al-Akmar, heard her crying and ran in to see what was wrong.

"Dear little sister, why are you crying? What's made you so unhappy?"

When she told him what had happened, he was angry at his father and promised his sister that he would stop this silly marriage. He went to his father to complain, but his words were wasted. The king could only think of the beautiful wooden horse.

"My son, you don't understand! This horse is amazing! Just try it and you'll see what I'm talking about!"

The king commanded his slaves to bring the horse for the prince to try. The prince was very good with horses, but when he got on this horse it wouldn't move. He sat on its back, kicking its sides and commanding it to move, but it just sat there, completely still. The king was very angry and ordered the wizard to show the prince how it worked. But the wizard had heard everything that the prince and the king had said and he was very angry at the prince for trying to stop his marriage. He came forward and, without smiling or even looking at the prince, pointed to a button on the horse's stomach, and said, "Press this."

The prince thought this man was quite rude, but he pressed the button. Suddenly the horse flew into the sky, higher and higher, until the prince and the horse were only a tiny spot. In the end the king couldn't see the horse or his son at all. He was very angry and told the wizard to make them come down again. But the wizard pretended that he was innocent.

"My Lord, there's nothing I can do! Your son was too silly and proud to ask me about the button for coming down and I'm afraid I forgot to tell him."

When the king heard this he was even angrier, so he ordered his slaves to put the wizard in prison. He then closed the doors of his palace and, with his wife and daughters and the rest of the people in the city, cried and cried for the prince they had lost.

While all this was happening, the horse kept flying nearer and nearer to the sun. The prince realized now that the wizard had heard his conversation with his father and had tricked him. He knew that he was completely lost and he regretted ever getting on the horse. But he was certain that if there was an "up" button, there must be a "down" button too. He kept feeling all over the horse until he found two buttons. He pressed one and the horse went faster and higher. So he quickly pressed the other one and the horse immediately began to slow down and fly toward the earth again.

When the prince realized that he had learned how to control the horse, he was very happy. He then began to play on the horse, making it go up and down and around in circles. He flew over cities and countries he had never seen before. One of these countries was especially beautiful, with green hills, clear streams, and many different types of animals. He came to a large city, which looked interesting. The sky was beginning to grow dark, so he decided to stay in that city for the night. He looked and looked for somewhere to land and eventually saw a tall palace. He pressed the "down" button and landed gently on the roof of the palace.

As the prince got down from the horse, he looked up at the sky and thanked Allah for his safe journey. He then carefully inspected the horse, which had given him such an amazing ride.

He couldn't believe how wonderful it was and thought to himself, "If this horse delivers me safely back to my father and family, I'll thank that funny-looking old wizard."

The prince was hungry and thirsty, but he waited on the roof until he was certain everyone would be asleep. He then went quietly down into the palace to find something to eat. When he was inside, he wandered through the different rooms and halls, admiring the beautiful architecture. He saw a light and found that it was outside a door, which was slightly open. There was a slave boy sleeping in front of the door, guarding the room. A large sword was lying on the floor by the slave's side and there was a leather bag next to him. The prince prayed to Allah to protect him and slowly and carefully took the leather bag and found some food inside. He ate quickly, returned the bag to its place, and stole the slave's sword.

The prince then went quietly through the door and saw a beautiful white bed. There were four slave girls sleeping on the white stone floor around the bed. A beautiful young woman was lying on the bed, also sleeping. Her hair was black and shone so brightly that it seemed to be full of stars. Her face and body were like a wonderful dream. The prince was so amazed by her beauty that he wasn't afraid. He went up to her, shaking with pleasure and excitement, and kissed her gently on her soft cheek. She immediately woke up with fear in her eyes.

"What's happening? Who are you?" she asked him.

"I'm your slave and your lover," the prince answered softly.

"And who sent you here?" she asked.

"Allah sent me," the prince replied.

The princess looked closely at this young man's face. He was very handsome and she was suddenly filled with love and desire. They began to talk, but although they were very quiet they woke the slave girls, who were very worried about the strange young man in their princess's bedroom.

"My princess. Who's this man and what's he doing here?" they asked.

"I'm afraid I have no idea who he is," replied the princess. "But he's very kind and charming."

Her answer worried the slave girls even more, so they rushed to get the slave boy who had been guarding the princess's door.

They woke him up and shouted at him angrily for allowing this stranger into the princess's room. The slave boy went for his sword, but it wasn't there. He ran to the princess's room and accused the prince of being an evil wizard because the prince had managed to get past him and into the princess's room.

"How dare you call me an evil wizard!" the prince shouted at the slave. "I am a royal prince! Your king married me to your princess and commanded me to come to my wife's room tonight!"

But the slave didn't believe this and ran to tell the king about the prince. The king wanted to kill the stupid slave for letting this happen. But he was also afraid for his daughter, so he rushed to her room. He met the slave girls at the door. They weren't sure if the prince was a man or an evil wizard either, but told the king that the young man had treated his daughter with respect.

When the king heard this, he relaxed a bit, looked into the room, and saw his daughter talking calmly to the prince. However, he still felt he had to protect his daughter's honor, so he ran into the room with his sword raised high.

"Young man!" he shouted. "You've damaged my daughter's honor by entering her room without permission from her king!"

"But my Lord," answered the prince, "it was an accident. I was wandering through your wonderful palace when I saw her great beauty. I'm afraid I couldn't control myself."

"Never mind that. I should have my slaves kill you right now!" the king shouted angrily. "You've damaged *my* honor as well as my daughter's. But instead of killing you now, we'll see how brave you really are. You say you're a royal prince. All right, you can keep your life until tomorrow. Then you must fight my army of 80,000 soldiers. If you fight my soldiers and win, you won't lose your life. And there's one more thing. I won't tell my army that you came into my daughter's room tonight. I'll tell them that you wish to marry my daughter and that I have commanded you to fight my army first. In this way, our honor will be saved."

"I accept your offer!" the prince said proudly. "And I'll win because my love for your daughter is true."

The prince was then taken to the king's room to sleep that night, so that the princess would be safe. The king and the prince sat for hours and talked about many things. The king began to like the prince. He thought he said very wise and intelligent things. He was also very brave. However, the king was certain that the prince would be killed in the next morning's battle. He was sad about this, but he knew that it was necessary in order to save his daughter's honor.

When morning came, the king's army gathered outside and the king spoke to his soldiers.

"Listen carefully. This young man has come to ask for permission to marry my daughter. I've never met a better young man, with a warmer heart or stronger spirit. He's told me that he can fight you and win. When the battle begins, you must attack him with all your strength."

Then he turned to the prince and told him to choose a horse and prepare for battle.

"I'm afraid, my lord, that none of your horses pleases me," replied the prince.

"What! These are the best horses in the country," the king replied. He was a little annoyed and felt that the prince was trying to make a fool of him again.

"My lord, I would prefer to ride my own horse, the horse I came on."

"And where is your horse?"

"On top of the palace."

"Where?"

"On the roof."

"What! Now you're being silly!" said the king. "People will think you're crazy. Maybe you *are* crazy!"

The king commanded his guards to go to the roof and bring down the prince's horse. When the soldiers got to the roof, they were surprised to see a beautiful black shining horse standing there. But as they came closer, they realized that it was a horse made of wood! They started laughing and agreed that the prince must be crazy. They lifted the horse and carried it down to the king.

After the shock of discovering that this was a wooden horse, the king admired its great beauty and asked the prince about it.

"Is this really your horse?"

"Oh yes!" the prince replied. "And you'll soon see just how amazing it is!"

"Well, it's time for the battle to begin. Get on your horse, Prince," the king ordered.

But the prince refused. "My Lord, your army is too close. I can't get on my horse until you command them to move back."

"And why is it necessary for me to move my army back?" the king asked with an annoyed look on his face.

"They might make my horse nervous, my Lord," answered the prince.

So the king commanded his soldiers to move back.

The prince then shouted, "Now watch, my Lord! I'm going to get on this horse and you'll find out how smart and strong we are. Together we'll destroy your army."

"Yes, yes! Just get on the horse!" shouted the king, who was beginning to lose his patience.

There were a few moments of silence as the prince climbed up onto the horse's shining back. Everyone was feeling tense as they waited for the battle to begin.

As soon as the prince was on his horse's back, he bent down and felt around the horse's stomach. All the people pushed each other to try to see what he was doing, not realizing that he had pressed the "up" button. At that moment the horse flew straight up into the sky!

When the king saw this, he shouted at his men, "Quick! Catch him before he escapes!"

But his soldiers were afraid and shouted back, "Oh, King, how can we catch a flying horse? This man must be an evil wizard! Oh Allah, please save us from him!"

Then people began to run in different directions, shouting in fear, "Allah, save us!"

After watching the prince's trick, the king rushed back to the palace and told his daughter what had happened. She became violently sick and fell on her bed crying. Her father had never seen his daughter so unhappy and tried to make her feel better.

"But dear daughter, we should be thankful that Allah has saved us from this wizard, who only wanted to make love to you!"

But he didn't realize how much his daughter loved the prince. She ignored her father's sympathetic words and told him that she wouldn't eat or drink until Allah brought her lover back to her. As the days passed, her condition became worse and worse. Her father was very worried and kept trying to help her, but she only loved the prince more and felt lonelier for him each day.

When Prince Kamar al-Akmar had flown high into the sky and knew he was safe, he turned his horse toward his own country. But as he flew toward his home, he could only think of the lovely princess. Her city was called Sana'a and he locked that name in his memory so he could return.

When he finally reached his own city, he came down to land on the roof of the palace. In the palace there was a great silence. The rooms were dark and empty. He thought that someone in his family had died, so he hurried into his father's room and found all his family dressed in black with sad, pale faces. When his father saw him, he shouted with joy and ran and put his arms around his son. Everyone cried with happiness and asked the prince what had happened to him. The prince told them about Sana'a, the princess, the king, and his soldiers.

"Praise to Allah for bringing you home safely, my son!" cried the king.

He sent messengers to give everyone the wonderful news. He then commanded his servants to prepare the palace and the city so that they could celebrate his son's return. The streets and markets were decorated and beautiful music was played. The king and queen threw their black clothes away and went out to meet their people. Everyone danced, sang, and ate and drank as much as they could for seven days and seven nights.

During this time the prince asked his father what had happened to the wizard who had invented the wooden horse. The king became angry when he remembered the wizard.

"He's an evil man and I was a fool to trust him. He's been in prison since the day you left us and he'll stay in prison forever."

But the prince told his father how amazing the horse was, and asked him to let the old man out of prison. The king finally agreed, but he wouldn't allow the man to marry his daughter.

When the wizard was freed and given this news, he was very angry. Although he had gotten his freedom back, he had lost his wonderful horse and his beautiful wife. He regretted giving the king the wooden horse.

As the people continued to celebrate, the king and his son returned to the palace to eat, drink, and talk together. Despite the fact that the prince had managed the horse so well, the king was worried and he tried to advise his son.

"I know that you've used this horse well, but you don't know everything about it. There could be hidden dangers. I think it would be a mistake for you to ride it again."

While they were sitting and talking in this way, a beautiful slave girl began to play music for them. She sang a song about separated lovers. As the prince listened to its sad words and beautiful music, the fire of love burned in his heart and he wanted the lovely daughter of the king of Sana'a more than ever. So when his father wasn't looking, he went quietly up to the roof, got on his horse, pressed the "up" button, and flew up into the night sky.

After a few hours the king wondered where his son had gone. When he couldn't find him anywhere in the palace, he went up to the roof and saw that the horse wasn't there.

"Oh Allah," he prayed, "please protect my son." And then he thought, "If my son returns to me, I'll definitely destroy that horse. Then the prince will have to stay here on the ground and I can stop worrying about him."

The prince flew through the night sky on his way to Sana'a and his love. When he arrived, he landed on the roof and went quietly down into the palace, where he again found the slave boy asleep in front of the princess's door. He listened through the door and heard the princess crying and talking to her slave girls.

"Princess, why are you crying about someone who left you and doesn't care about you?"

"You silly girl! You don't really believe that he's forgotten me or that I could forget him, do you?"

And she began to cry again until she finally fell asleep.

The prince's heart was full of joy when he heard the princess's words, so he climbed over the sleeping slave boy, walked quietly up to her bed, and touched her hand gently. The princess opened her eyes when she felt his touch and threw herself on him, kissing him a hundred times.

"Oh, I've been so unhappy!" she cried.

"I've been unhappy too," the prince answered.

"Then why did you leave?" she cried. "If you had stayed away one day longer, I would have killed myself!"

"How could I stay here when your father hated me?"

"But you were wrong to leave me! Did you really believe I could live without you?"

The prince begged the princess to forget all the bad things that had happened and to try to be happy that they were finally together again. The princess ordered her slave girls to bring food and drink, and the prince ate and drank happily after his long journey. They then talked until the sun rose over the palace walls.

When morning came, they both realized that they couldn't be separated again. But her father would never allow them to marry, so they made secret preparations to leave the palace together.

The princess put on her finest clothes and jewels and, while her slave girls were sleeping, she quietly left her room and went up to the roof with the prince. He climbed up onto the horse, helped the princess up, and tied her tightly to him with a strong rope.

He then turned to his love and asked, "My Princess, are you sure you want to leave your home and your family?"

She answered, "My love for you is so strong that I can think of nothing else. If I have to choose between you and my family, then you are the only possible choice."

The prince felt better and pressed the "up" button. The wooden horse immediately flew high up into the sky.

They kept flying until they came to the prince's city. The prince was very happy to see his home again. He left his princess in one of his father's beautiful gardens, telling her to stay there and watch the horse carefully. He then went to his father and asked him to prepare a beautiful royal ceremony to welcome the princess. His father was very happy to see his son again and immediately ordered his servants to prepare for the arrival of the princess.

The prince then went back to get the princess but was shocked to discover that she and the horse were both gone. One of his guards told him that he had seen an ugly old man in the garden earlier. The prince realized that the wizard had taken the princess and the horse. He hurried to his father and told him what had happened and that he had to find the princess. The king was very upset and begged his son not to leave them again, but the prince wouldn't listen and left to search for his princess.

The prince had been right. The wizard had captured the princess and taken her away with him on the wooden horse. The princess cried and cried as the horse flew through the sky.

Eventually they came to the land of the Greeks and the wizard stopped to rest in a green field with trees and clear water. The field was very near a large city. The king of that city was out hunting that day and found the horse, the old man, and the princess. He wondered why this beautiful princess was traveling with this ugly old man, so he asked her about their relationship. The wizard tried to say that the princess was his wife, but she told the king that the wizard had forced her to go with him. When he heard this, the king commanded his soldiers to throw the wizard into prison. The king took the princess with him and put the beautiful horse with his other treasures in a special room in his palace.

While all this was happening, the prince was traveling from country to country, asking people if they had seen the princess and the magic horse. He eventually arrived in the land of the Greeks and heard some merchants talking in the market about the king's discovery of the princess, the old man, and the horse. He joined the group and discovered that the old man was in prison and that the princess and the horse were in the king's palace.

He immediately traveled to the palace, but it was too late for the guards to take him to the king, so they decided to put him in prison for the night. But first, because he was such a pleasant young man, they shared their meal with him. They started talking and asked him where he was from. When he told them he was from Persia, they laughed and said that all Persians told terrible lies.

"And the worst of you is in our prison right now! He says he's a wizard. When the king found him, he had a beautiful young woman and an amazing wooden horse with him. The king has fallen in love with the woman, but she's completely crazy. If this old man was really a wizard he could save her, but he can't. The king has spent almost all his money this past year on doctors to try to cure her, but nothing has worked. The horse is locked away in a special room and the old man is locked up in this prison."

Finally it was time for the guards to lock the prince up for the night. As he sat in his cell, he heard the old man crying and talking to himself in the next cell.

The prince shouted at him, "Be quiet! Do you think you're the only person who has problems?"

But the old man was so happy to have some company that he told this young stranger his whole story. He didn't realize that this was the prince he had tricked so badly.

As the prince sat there in the darkness, listening to the wizard's complaints, he had an idea for freeing his princess. The next morning, when the guards took him to meet the king, the prince told the king that he was a doctor from Persia who traveled the world helping sick and crazy people. The king became very excited.

"Oh, doctor, I'm so happy to meet you," he said. "And you've come just in time! Thanks to Allah!" He then told the prince all about the princess and the horse. "If you can cure my princess,

I'll give you anything you desire in payment!" he promised the prince happily.

So the prince agreed to treat the princess. He told the king that he would have to examine the wooden horse because he would need it for the treatment. So the king took him to see the horse. The prince inspected it carefully and found that it was in perfect condition.

The prince then went with the king to the princess's room. The king waited outside while the prince went in to examine the princess. The princess was crying, screaming, and waving her arms around wildly. The prince knew that she was just pretending so people would stay away from her.

As he came slowly toward her, he tried to make her relax. "Please don't worry. Nobody's going to hurt you, my beauty." When he was by her side, he whispered in her ear. "It's me. Kamar Al-Akmar."

As soon as she heard this, the princess screamed and fainted with joy.

The king was very worried and shouted through the door, "What's going on in there? Have you frightened her? Are you all right, my Princess?"

The prince quickly whispered again in his princess's ear. "Oh, Shams al-Nahar, be careful. We're in great danger. We must plan everything carefully so we can escape. I'll go outside your room and tell the king that you're crazy because the wizard put an evil spirit into the wooden horse, which then got into you. Then I'll tell him that I can remove this evil spirit and cure you. When I've finished, I'll come back into your room and talk to you for a few moments. Afterward I'll invite the king in. You must then talk very sweetly to him to make him believe that my treatment has made you better."

When the prince had finally done all these things, he invited the king into the princess's room. The princess smiled warmly at him and welcomed him with a kiss. The king was very happy and thanked the "doctor" with all his heart. The prince then told the king that the princess was not completely well yet.

"In order to complete the cure," the prince explained, "you and your soldiers must take the princess and the wooden horse back to the place where you found her. I will only then be able to remove the evil spirit from the horse and destroy it completely. If I don't do that, it will continue to drive the princess crazy."

The king agreed. He now thought the doctor was so intelligent and honest that he believed anything he said.

The soldiers took the horse to the field, followed by the king and the princess. The prince, still dressed like a doctor, gave the king his orders.

"My Lord, this could be dangerous, so first you must put the princess and the horse as far away as possible from you and your soldiers. I will then go and remove the evil spirit from the horse. I will get on the horse and put the princess behind me. The horse will shake and make strange noises. But don't worry—this is a necessary part of the treatment. The horse will turn and run straight toward you and your soldiers. When this happens, you'll know that the evil spirit has been completely removed from the horse. You may then do whatever you want with the princess."

When the king heard this, he was very happy. He quickly ordered his army to move back from the princess and the horse. The prince left the king and walked slowly to the horse. He climbed up onto the horse's back, helped the princess up, and tied her tightly to him. He then reached down and pressed the "up" button. The horse immediately flew up into the air, higher and higher into the sky, until it could be seen no more. The king and his soldiers stood there silently watching. They stood that way for half a day, waiting for the horse to return.

Eventually the king realized that he had been a fool. He knew that there was nothing he could do, so slowly and sadly he returned to his palace.

The prince flew day and night until he finally arrived at his father's palace. After landing on the roof and making sure that the princess was safely inside, he went to see his father and mother. They were full of joy when they saw him, and the servants prepared the palace and the city so that everyone could celebrate the return of the prince and princess. People then celebrated for thirty days and nights, with delicious food, beautiful music, and dancing in the streets.

At the end of the thirty days, the prince married his lovely princess and they enjoyed each other with great happiness on their wedding night. King Sabur destroyed the horse so his son could never leave again and get into trouble. He then wrote to the princess's father to tell him that she was safe and happily married.

The king of Sana'a was filled with joy to hear this news. He sent messages of friendship and many expensive gifts back to his daughter, her new husband, and their family. Prince Kamar Al-Akmar was very happy to receive his good wishes and invited him to the palace.

After many happy years, King Sabur died and Prince Kamar Al-Akmar became king. He was a good, kind king and his people loved him.

The Wedding Box

In a small town in China called Teng-chou lived a widow called Mrs. Hsüeh. Her husband had been a smart businessman and Mrs. Hsüeh was now quite wealthy from the money he had left her. She had only one child, a daughter called Hsüeh Hsiang-ling. Hsiang-ling was a beautiful girl with many talents. Mrs. Hsüeh loved her and wanted the best for her. She always gave her daughter whatever she desired. She didn't realize that Hsiang-ling had become spoiled.

The years seemed to fly past, until one night Mrs. Hsüeh looked at her daughter and saw that she wasn't a little girl now. She was sixteen years old, a young woman ready for marriage. Mrs. Hsüeh arranged for her to marry a young man from a wealthy family in another town. She then began to prepare for her daughter's wedding. It was the tradition that a young woman took gifts of property and money to her new husband. Mrs. Hsüeh prepared all of this with great care. She wanted her daughter to go to her new home with pride.

Mrs. Hsüeh then began preparing her own gift for her daughter. She went to the most expensive store in the town to order a wedding box. The box would be covered in bright red silk and would have a colorful *ch'i-lin* sewn on the top. A *ch'i-lin* is an animal that all Chinese people know from ancient stories. A wedding box with this animal on it would promise the birth of a strong and smart son. This would be Mrs. Hsüeh's special gift to her daughter on her wedding day.

However, it was very difficult to buy anything that would please Hsiang-ling. The color was wrong, or maybe the size; you could be sure that anything her mother bought would have to be exchanged or returned to the store. When the box was ready and the family servant brought it home from the store, Hsiang-ling wasn't satisfied at all. She inspected it with a cold look on her face and said, "I don't like the *ch'i-lin*. The design is all wrong. Take it back to the store."

So the servant returned to the store, told them what Hsiang-ling had said, and ordered another box. But when he brought the second box home, she was still unhappy. The colors were too dark. A third box was ordered but this still didn't please her.

Finally, the servant got very upset. "I can't do this again," he cried. "The people in the store laughed at me the last time. They told me that I'm difficult to please, but it's not me. *You* are the difficult one! You're never satisfied! I'm afraid that if you don't want this box, there's nothing I can do. I'll have to leave and work for another family."

Although Hsiang-ling was spoiled, she was not a bad person. She began to feel sorry for the servant. He was an old man and had been a loyal servant to their family since before she was born. So she agreed to keep the box and told him to go back to the store and pay for it. The servant was grateful that she had changed her mind because he didn't really want to leave the family. He went back to the store, paid for the box, and gave it to Mrs. Hsüeh so she could fill it with gifts for her daughter.

The sixteenth day of the eighth month arrived and it was time for Hsiang-ling's wedding. Hsiang-ling had been looking forward to this day for many months. Her excitement had grown as she watched her mother preparing all the wonderful gifts and her beautiful wedding clothes. But she also felt sad because she knew she was leaving her mother.

Early in the morning her mother helped Hsiang-ling put on her beautiful wedding dress of the finest red silk. She was then taken to her *hua-chiao*. The *hua-chiao* is a special chair which is used to take a woman to her new husband. She sits in the *hua-chiao* and curtains are closed around her so she can't be seen. The chair is then carried on the shoulders of four strong men. Hsiang-ling's *hua-chiao* had beautiful red silk curtains.

Mrs. Hsüeh lifted the curtain at the front of the *hua-chiao* to speak to her daughter one last time before she left.

"This is your special day, my daughter, and I'm so proud and happy that you look so beautiful and that you're marrying such a fine young man. Here's my gift to you, a wedding box. When you're in your new home, open it and you'll see all the nice gifts I've put inside. I hope that when you do this, you'll feel my love for you."

But Hsiang-ling wasn't really listening. She was too busy thinking about her wedding and wondering what her husband, whom she had never met, would be like. She kissed her mother, took the box, and put it by her side. A few minutes later the four men came, picked up the *hua-chiao*, and Hsiang-ling's journey to her new life began.

As they came to the main road, it started to rain. Soon it was raining so hard that the road became a sea of mud and it wasn't safe to continue. So the men carried the *hua-chiao* into a shelter at the side of the road to wait for the storm to end.

Hsiang-ling was annoyed by the rain and anxious to get to her new home. Then she heard something. Was someone crying? Or was it the sound of the rain? She opened her curtain to see. In the shelter, next to hers, was another *hua-chiao*. It wasn't nearly as nice as hers, and it had old, torn curtains. And yes, the crying was coming from inside the old *hua-chiao*. This only annoyed Hsiang-ling more.

"Why is this woman so unhappy on her wedding day? This could bring me bad luck!" she thought.

So she sent her servant to find out what was wrong with the girl. The servant came back and told Hsiang-ling that the young woman was very sad because she was poor and had nothing to take to her new home.

Hsiang-ling then felt sorry for her. She realized that she had always had everything she wanted and that this girl had nothing.

It was especially sad because it was her wedding day. Hsiang-ling didn't have any money with her, so she decided to give her the box. She called her servant again.

"Here. Take this to her, but don't tell her who sent it. Don't tell her my name."

The servant tried to stop her. "But Hsüeh Hsiang-ling, this is your wedding box!"

"Shhsh! I don't care. Take it to her now. Quickly!" Hsiang-ling ordered.

The servant did as she was told and went quickly to give the box to the girl. The crying immediately stopped, leaving only the sound of the rain.

Soon the storm ended and the men picked up the *hua-chiao* to start again on their journey. Hsiang-ling had given a stranger her wedding box without knowing what her dear mother had put inside.

In a few hours she arrived at her new home and the marriage took place that evening. She discovered that her mother had chosen well for her. Her husband was a wonderful and handsome young man. After a year of marriage they had a beautiful, healthy baby boy. Hsiang-ling felt that she must be the happiest woman in the world.

But after six years this happiness was destroyed when a terrible flood hit their area. Hsiang-ling and her family lost their home and everything they owned. In the rush to escape the town, Hsiang-ling became separated from her husband and little boy in the crowds. She searched and searched but she couldn't find them anywhere. So she finally had to accept defeat and travel with other people who were escaping to a town called Lai-chou. It was a long, difficult journey and Hsiang-ling was full of sorrow. She didn't think she would ever see her husband and child again.

Life was hard when they first reached Lai-chou, so everyone tried to help each other. One day, as Hsiang-ling sat, exhausted and alone, by the side of the road, a woman came up to her and said, "You look terrible. And you must be hungry. You can find food not too far from here, just down this road. Yüan-wai Lu, a wealthy businessman, has put up a tent and his servant is giving food to people who've suffered in the flood. Go now. I'm sure you can get something to eat there."

Hsiang-ling thanked the woman and went to find this place. When she got there, she found a long line of people holding bowls and silently waiting. Hsiang-ling had never done anything like this before in her life. She had never felt so depressed. As she was standing there, holding her bowl and waiting for her turn, she had to force back her tears.

Finally her turn came. Yüan-wai Lu's servant put the last bit of food into Hsiang-ling's bowl and then announced to the rest of the people in the line that there was no more food left and they should come back tomorrow. The person behind her began to cry. Hsiang-ling turned around and saw an older woman. When she looked at this woman, she remembered her mother. She thought of how much she loved her and how unselfish she had been. Without saying anything, she put her food into the woman's bowl and walked away. She couldn't stop her tears now and they ran down her cheeks until she could hardly see where she was going.

The servant had watched all of this. He was very surprised at what Hsiang-ling had done and ran after her. As she was walking away, Hsiang-ling heard him shouting.

"Madam! Madam! Please stop!"

Hsiang-ling stopped and turned around. The servant then asked her why she had given her food to the woman.

She said simply, "I'm very hungry, but I'm also young. I can stand my hunger for longer than that old woman can."

The servant smiled. "Well, you did a very unselfish thing. My employer, Yüan-wai Lu, is looking for someone like you to take care of his young son. Are you interested in this job?"

"Oh, yes. Thank you," Hsiang-ling replied, feeling happier.

"Then come with me now," the servant told her. He then took her to Yüan-wai Lu's house.

When Yüan-wai Lu met Hsiang-ling and heard the servant's story of her great kindness, he offered her the job immediately.

He then told Hsiang-ling, "My wife is an excellent mother but unfortunately has had very poor health for some years. This is why we need someone to take care of our young son. You will have a lot of freedom in this job, but there's one place you must never go. That is the small house at the end of our garden. It is my wife's private place. If I ever discover that you've been inside, you'll lose your job immediately. On this one point I must be very clear."

Hsiang-ling agreed to this and began her new life. She liked the little boy. It didn't take long, however, for her to discover that he was very spoiled. He wanted everything immediately and if he didn't get what he wanted, he cried and cried until he did. This upset Hsiang-ling because it reminded her of how spoiled she had been as a child. She regretted now how badly she had behaved.

One day she and the little boy were playing in the garden when his ball went into the little house. The boy began to cry.

"I want my ball! Go and get it!" he shouted.

Hsiang-ling told him that she wasn't allowed inside the house, but the boy didn't care and just cried louder. She tried again to make him understand.

"But your father doesn't allow this. If I go in there, I'll lose my job."

The boy wasn't listening. His face was red and wet with tears. He started screaming.

Hsiang-ling finally gave up and agreed to go inside. She looked around to make sure no one could see her and then walked quietly up the steps, opened the door, and stepped inside.

When her eyes became used to the darkness, she was very surprised by what she saw. It was a temple, calm and peaceful. She walked slowly toward a small table, which was covered with a beautiful yellow silk cloth. On the table was a small Buddha, some pictures of relatives from long ago, and there, in the middle of all this, was her wedding box! She couldn't believe what she was seeing.

Hsiang-ling remembered her wedding day and how happy she had been. She thought of her mother's love and kindness. She thought of her husband and her son and how much she missed them. She had had everything and now she had nothing. She started crying so hard that her body shook.

Suddenly someone touched her shoulder. Shocked, she quickly turned around and saw a woman's angry face. It was Mrs. Lu, the wife of her employer. A young servant girl was standing behind her.

"What are you doing here?" asked Mrs. Lu angrily.

"I'm so sorry," Hsiang-ling answered. "Your son's ball came in here. He was very unhappy. He wouldn't stop crying. In the end I felt I had to do as he asked and get his ball for him. Forgive me, please. I know that this is your private place."

"Why were you crying?" asked Mrs. Lu.

"Because I saw the box, my wedding box. My mother gave me this box on my wedding day."

Mrs. Lu looked shocked. "Where are you from?" she asked, as she picked up the box and sat down in a chair near the table. Her voice now sounded strange, almost happy.

"I'm from Teng-chou," answered Hsiang-ling.

"What was your name before you were married?" Mrs. Lu asked.

"Hsüeh Hsiang-ling."

Mrs. Lu said nothing to Hsiang-ling, but turned to her servant girl. "Bring her a chair," she ordered.

The servant wasn't happy at all about bringing a chair for another servant, but she did as she was asked.

Mrs. Lu then told Hsiang-ling to sit down on the chair. Hsiang-ling was surprised to be treated with such honor. She didn't understand, but she was afraid to speak.

"And when were you married?"

"On the sixteenth day of the eighth month, six years ago."

Mrs. Lu was silent for a moment. Her face looked very strange now. Could she be smiling?

"Tell me. How did you lose this box?" she asked.

Hsiang-ling then told Mrs. Lu about the terrible rain storm on her wedding day, the old *hua-chiao*, and the sad young woman.

Suddenly, Mrs. Lu went down on her knees in front of Hsiang-ling and began to cry.

"You saved me!" she cried with joy. "Your kindness on my wedding day took away my worry and brought me so much joy. All these years I've been praying for your health and happiness. When I got to my new home, I opened your box and found many things of great value inside, including this beautiful piece of the finest jade."

She took a piece of deep green jade out of the small box and held it up for Hsiang-ling to see.

"When my husband and I were first married, we didn't have much money. I took this jade to the moneylender and received a large payment for it. That allowed us to start a business, which has made us very rich. As soon as we had enough money, I went to the moneylender and bought the jade back. I've kept it in this box since that time. I didn't know how to find you, so I built this temple to honor you. I've always hoped and prayed that we would meet. I'm so grateful that I can now thank you with all my heart. So please take your box. Your mother must be a wonderful person because she gave you such a special gift on your wedding day."

Hsiang-ling cried with happiness as Mrs. Lu put the box into her hands.

Mrs. Lu then spoke again. "I know that your husband and son are missing. We'll send people out to search for them immediately. I also want you to think about something else. When your family returns, we would like to share our property with you. Please accept this. You'll make us very happy if you do."

That same day Yüan-wai Lu sent servants out to search for Hsiang-ling's husband and son. They were soon found, not far from Teng-chou. The two families lived near each other from that time and became very close friends. They were always ready to help each other.

As the years went by and Hsiang-ling grew older, she often told the story of the wedding box. She always ended her story with these words: "Remember, life moves in circles and happiness comes to people who help others."

The Golden Apples

Very early one summer morning the gods Odin, Honir, and Loki left their world, Asgard, the world of the gods, and crossed the flaming bridge over the ocean into Midgard, the world of men. They were exploring, hoping to find some land that they had never seen before. In the blue light of early morning they walked over the rough, rocky ground of Midgard. There was nothing here, no trees to protect them from the cold, stinging winds.

All day they walked until they came to an ice-cold river, which ran down from a mountain into a small valley. They followed the river into the valley and made preparations to camp that night. They were beginning to worry, as they had brought no food with them and had seen no animals to hunt. So while Odin and Honir gathered wood and built a fire, Loki went hunting and managed to kill two wild pigs for their dinner. They cut the pigs into large pieces, threw the pieces onto the fire, and waited. Although the sun still hadn't set, the heat had gone out of the summer's day. The gods sat close to the fire, warming themselves and waiting for food to fill their empty stomachs. The smell of the meat made them crazy with hunger.

After some time Honir took a piece of meat from the fire with his spear, but just as he was preparing to put it into his mouth he saw that it wasn't cooked. The inside was still the color of blood. He threw it onto the ground and the other two inspected it. This was very strange, but they realized that they were in a different world and that maybe things took longer. So they put the piece of meat back on the fire and waited. They waited and waited, but after several hours the meat still hadn't cooked.

"There must be a power working against us," said Odin.

At that exact moment they heard a loud scream coming from above them. Shocked, they looked up and saw an enormous eagle sitting in a tree. When they had gotten their voices back, they asked him what he wanted.

"Nothing more than food in my stomach," the eagle replied. "If you share your meat with me, I will allow it to cook."

The gods agreed. They knew they had no choice. The eagle then spread its enormous wings, flew down, and settled by the fire. They waited for a short time without speaking, the gods watching the eagle carefully. When the meat was at last cooked, the eagle reached into the fire, took each piece of meat in its claws, and ate until he had finished it all. The gods were very angry, but they were also helpless. This wasn't their land and they could do nothing. Their powers were of no use here.

But Loki couldn't control his anger. He jumped to his feet, raised his spear, and drove it deep into the eagle's body. The eagle was thrown backward and gave a long, loud cry of pain. He then suddenly and violently flew into the air with one end of Loki's spear in his side. Loki discovered that he was unable to let go of the other end.

The eagle flew at great speed close to the ground, dragging the terrified Loki across the sharp rocks of Midgard. Loki screamed with pain and begged the eagle to let him go, but the eagle ignored him and only flew faster, as the cold, sharp ice cut Loki's knees and ankles. Again Loki begged. He thought his arms were going to be pulled out of his body. He was crying like a baby now. He couldn't breathe, he was in so much pain.

"Let me go!" he cried. "Please let me go!"

"I'll free you only if you promise me," shouted the eagle.

"Promise you what?"

"You must do something for me."

"What? Do what? I'll do anything. I can't stand this! You're killing me!" was Loki's desperate reply.

"I will free you if, in seven days, you bring the goddess Idun and her apples out of Asgard. Bring her to me. Do you hear me?"

Loki said nothing. He realized now that the eagle was really a giant. The giants were the ancient enemies of the gods. The eagle suddenly flew down, banging Loki's body against the ground again and again.

"All right! All right!" shouted Loki. "I will do this! Just let me go!"

The eagle immediately freed Loki and he dropped to the ground like a rock. He lay there for some time, exhausted and unable to think because of the pain. He then got to his feet and struggled back to where Odin and Honir were camped. He described his horrible experience but he didn't tell them about the promise he had made to the eagle.

Seven days later, without telling anyone where he was going, Loki went to get Idun, as he had promised. Idun was the wife of the god Bragi. She was the gentlest of the goddesses, the goddess of poetry. She never worried about the wars and silly arguments of others. She was like an innocent child who had never experienced evil. She sang as she did her daily jobs and always gave comfort to others when they were worried or frightened. And, of course, there were her apples, the golden apples which contained the gift of never-ending youth. She carried them with her always, in her basket.

On this day Loki found Idun walking in the fields near her home, singing and gathering flowers. He ran up to her shouting, "Idun! I've come as quickly as I could. I had to tell you!"

"Dear Loki, tell me what?"

"About the tree, the tree I saw in Midgard. It . . . it's in a forest . . . and it shines . . . like the sun . . . and on its branches are the most beautiful golden apples, just like yours! And they also contain the gift of never-ending youth! I think we must take these for our gods, don't you?"

If someone else had heard Loki's story, they would have had doubts. It was never wise to trust him. He was exciting, handsome, and smart but also unfaithful, selfish, and always ready to cheat you. It was easy for him to play tricks because he had the power to change his shape, even his sex. But Idun trusted everyone, so she believed Loki's story.

"Of course, if you think so," she replied.

"And don't forget to bring your apples so we can compare them. I could be wrong. I only saw the tree for a moment and then ran to tell you!"

So Idun, with her basket of apples, hurried with Loki to the place where he had told her the tree would be. The eagle was waiting for them. As they approached, it rose from behind a rock, spread its enormous wings, took hold of Idun in its powerful claws, and flew with her and her apples over the wide sea toward Jotunheim, the land of the giants. This proved to Loki that the eagle was really a giant. It was the giant Thiazi.

Thiazi took Idun to Jotunheim, high in the mountains. His house, Thrymheim, seemed to grow out of the cold, dark rock. Here he kept Idun prisoner so that, without the apples, the gods would grow old—but he would stay young forever.

Back in Asgard, when they realized that Idun was missing, the gods became extremely worried. They knew that without her golden apples they would grow old, and that quickly began to happen. They grew smaller inside their clothes and deep lines appeared on their faces. Their skin became so thin that it seemed that their bones would break through. Hands shook, knees made cracking noises, hair fell out in handfuls. The gods felt the lightness in their walk and the strength in their bodies leaving them as the hours passed.

Then the minds of the gods began to suffer. One began to complain about the faults of the others. Another began to talk nonsense. But mostly they just became quiet. When they did speak, they repeated themselves or began sentences which they didn't finish. They all shared the same deep fear, the fear that they were growing old and would soon die. But although they knew they were in terrible trouble, they couldn't think clearly.

Odin knew he had to force himself to be strong. He was the most powerful, the strongest, the oldest of all the gods. He had created heaven, the earth, the sky, and everything in them. He was the one-eyed god of war, terrible and terrifying. But others expected answers from him. He was their leader. He called a meeting of the gods in his great hall to decide what to do. Everyone slowly struggled to the meeting, some using sticks to help them walk. It was a sad sight.

When they had all gathered, only Loki and Idun were missing. Odin told the crowd that they must find Idun and asked who had last seen her. A servant told them he had seen Loki leading Idun out of Asgard. A deep silence fell over the meeting. Everyone knew that Loki must be the cause of what had happened to them. They agreed that they would have to find him.

Despite the fact that they were exhausted and had terrible aches and pains, they searched everywhere. When at last they found Loki sleeping peacefully in Idun's field, he was taken to Odin's great hall and accused of leading Idun out of Asgard.

"Unless you return Idun with her apples to us before the second sunset, you will be killed," Odin threatened.

Loki tried to get himself out of trouble. He told them that the eagle was really the giant, Thiazi. Then he described what Thiazi had done to him.

"I was lucky to escape from him alive! I had no choice. I had to promise to take Idun to him!" he cried.

"But you did not have to *keep* this promise!" Odin's voice was like thunder. "If you love eagles so much, we will burn an eagle onto your back!"

Loki dropped to the ground in fear. "No! No!" he shouted. "I'll go and get her. But I'll need Freyja's falcon skin so I can fly over the wide sea to Jotunheim."

Odin agreed, so Loki followed the goddess Freyja to get her magic falcon skin, which gave anyone who wore it the power of flight. They walked slowly. Loki had to help Freyja several times. Freyja had once been the most beautiful goddess, the goddess of love, desired by everyone. But now the skin on her face hung like an old leather bag. Her body, which used to be so lovely, was now thin and sad. Her golden hair was falling out.

"You're not so beautiful now that you're losing your hair," said Loki with a smile.

Freyja said nothing. Tears of gold ran down her cheeks. She handed her falcon skin to Loki.

Loki put on the skin and became a falcon, with the strength to fly long distances. He flew over the wide sea to Jotunheim and found Thiazi's house in the mountains. He discovered Idun alone in a room filled with smoke from a small fire. She was sitting by the fire, trying to warm herself. There were tears in her eyes. Luckily, Thiazi had gone out hunting.

Loki climbed into the room and before Idun could even speak, he whispered the magic words and turned her into a tiny stone. He picked her up in his claws and flew away as fast as he could. When Thiazi returned and discovered that Idun was gone, he put on his eagle skin and flew across the sky, over the dark mountains, chasing after Loki.

Odin sat in his great hall looking over the nine worlds. Nothing could escape his sight. His one eye could see things that no other gods could see. He saw Loki flying back to Asgard with Idun. He also saw Thiazi chasing Loki. So he ordered the gods to prepare an enormous fire by the walls of Asgard, but not to light it until Loki was home again. As soon as Loki flew over the walls and into Asgard, they lit the fire. The flames rose up. The eagle, who was close behind Loki, couldn't stop in time and flew straight into the fire. His wings began to burn and he fell to the ground in terrible pain. The gods rushed forward and killed him.

Loki then threw off Freyja's falcon skin and became himself again. He looked around at the old, gray, anxious faces and laughed at them. Then he brought out the small stone and spoke the magic words. Idun appeared, young, gentle, and smiling. The gods cried with happiness. Idun was shocked by the way they looked and immediately took out her basket and offered them her apples. As each apple was taken from the basket, another appeared in its place. The gods and goddesses looked at each other with wonder in their eyes as the apples brought back their youth and beauty.

While all this was happening, Loki silently left the group. They would come after him later. They would punish him. He knew that. And he would hurt them again. But that was how it was.

Happy New Year

Six hundred years ago, on a cold winter's night, Mrs. Yeh sat alone in her living room, waiting for her husband, Mr. Yeh, to return. He had been gone for almost a year, teaching in a private school about seventy kilometers away. Mrs. Yeh was looking forward to seeing him. She also needed the salary he had earned for his year of work. All the money he had left her was now gone and New Year's Eve was approaching, a very special but expensive holiday.

New Year's Eve dinner was the most important meal of the year, even more important than New Year's Day. The Chinese believed that a New Year's Eve dinner with plenty of delicious, healthy food would start the year well and bring them happiness and wealth. A typical New Year's Eve meal included four "wholes"—a whole chicken, a whole duck, a whole fish, and a whole leg of pork—and four kinds of cold meat. Then there was also a sweet rice dish with eight different things in it, and the "eight specials," which is made of eight different kinds of vegetables and beans.

The New Year's holiday lasted for fifteen days, and if people could afford it they cooked enough food for the whole two weeks. This allowed them to relax and visit relatives and friends without having to think about cooking. But more importantly, it showed other people that they were wealthy enough to buy all this food. So this time of year was important for everyone's pride.

Mrs. Yeh began to worry, as she had expected her husband home hours ago. She tried not to think about possible disasters that could happen on a winter's night like this, with the terrible snow and ice. At last she heard footsteps coming along the path. She hurried to open the door and there, shaking the snow off his cap, was her husband, Mr. Yeh.

Mrs. Yeh gave her husband a bowl of hot soup to drink by the fire. Later, when he finally felt his body warming from the fire and the soup, she asked him about his salary.

"Well, was it a good year?"

"Yes, it was. I earned a silver *yüan-pao*,"★ he answered.

"Oh! Thank Buddha. Now we can enjoy our New Year's Eve dinner. So where is this silver *yüan-pao*? Let's put it in the money pot and I'll make some tea."

Mr. Yeh hesitated and then said quietly, "Well, there's one small problem."

"What problem?" his wife asked.

"I gave it away," he answered.

"What! Oh, old man. Don't joke with a poor old woman after a hard year. Where is the *yüan-pao*? Give it to me."

"I'm afraid I'm not joking," Mr. Yeh said in a serious voice. "Please bring me some hot tea and I'll tell you what happened." He then sat there warming his hands on his teacup. "It all started when I was walking along the road. I was feeling very happy that I was coming home . . ." And so he began his story.

It was freezing cold and he had to pull his old coat up around his face to help keep out the cold wind. But he was happy too because in his bag he had his silver *yüan-pao*. He was sure that his wife had used all the money she had and was "waiting for rice to put into the pot," as they say in China. He couldn't wait to get home and see the joy in her eyes when he gave her the silver *yüan-pao*. He was also happy because it was almost New Year's Eve, his favorite holiday. As he walked along, he started to plan the menu for the New Year's Eve dinner. He knew that they would probably not be able to buy four "wholes." But at least his wife could get some pork and cook his favorite meal, pork with

★*yüan-pao*: silver and gold money used in ancient China

red wine and red beans. He would get out his favorite rice wine to have with it.

Suddenly, as he was walking along thinking these happy thoughts, he saw a woman running toward the river. He was sure she was going to throw herself in. As he struggled to see better through the falling snow, he realized it was A-ken Sao, the wife of the carpenter A-ken. He rushed forward to stop her and just managed to catch her in his arms before she got to the water.

"Let me go! Please!" she cried.

But he refused. "You can't end your life like this! What is it? What's wrong?"

"Let me die, please," cried A-ken Sao. "I haven't heard from A-ken for a whole year. He's either died or left me, but I must pay the rent by tomorrow. If I don't, the owner of the building is going to sell our daughter, Yeng-hua! But I have no money! I can't pay the rent! There's nothing I can do!"

"No! You're wrong. A-ken did write to you," said Mr. Yeh. He was thinking hard.

A-ken Sao stopped struggling. "Oh, do you have a letter for me then?"

"Um . . . well . . . I . . ." said Mr. Yeh. He let go of her and pretended to search in his pockets. After a minute, he smiled and apologized. "Sorry, I thought I had a letter. I'm sure there was a letter."

"Oh!" cried A-ken Sao, and she started to run toward the river again.

Mr. Yeh shouted, "No! Wait! I was confused. I made a mistake. A-ken didn't give me a letter but he did send some money for you."

He took his silver *yüan-pao* out of his bag, looked at it one last time, and gave it to A-ken Sao.

She stopped and looked down for a quiet moment at the silver *yüan-pao* in her hand. A wide smile appeared on her face and then she began to laugh.

"Oh! My husband is alive and hasn't forgotten us! And our daughter has been saved! Thank Buddha!" she cried happily. "And thank you too, Mr. Yeh. I must go to my daughter. Thank you! Thank you so much!" She was crying again now, but with happiness, as she ran away down the road.

"Watching her, I knew I'd just given our New Year's Eve dinner away," Mr. Yeh told his wife, who was sitting opposite him at their table. "But what could I do?" Mr. Yeh was very depressed.

"But why did you give A-ken Sao *all* your money?" Mrs. Yeh asked. "Why didn't you save some for us?"

"I had only one *yüan-pao*. I'd told her that this *yüan-pao* was A-ken's salary, which he'd asked me to give her."

Mrs. Yeh became angry. "But what's going to happen to us now? Do we have to die of hunger because of your kindness? You must do something. We need food. I want you to ask our friends and neighbors for the same kindness. Go and borrow some money for our New Year's food."

Mr. Yeh knew he couldn't refuse his wife, so he did as she asked. The next morning, he went out to ask their neighbors if he could borrow some money. He knew that New Year's Eve was the worst time to do this. People were busy cooking dinner, and they believed that people who borrowed money could bring them bad luck in the New Year. Almost every door was shut in his face. Finally one man gave him a small package, but when he opened it he discovered that it was only stones wrapped in some paper.

Tired and disappointed, Mr. Yeh went home and told his wife he had failed. "I'm exhausted," he said. "Let's go to bed and not think about dinner. We have nothing to eat anyway. I'll try to think of something in the morning."

But his wife was too hungry to sleep. "No, you have to do something," she told him. "I have an idea. The fields are full of big sweet potatoes at the moment. Why don't you get some of those?"

"But those potatoes don't belong to us. Those aren't our fields," Mr. Yeh replied.

"So?"

"What? You want me to steal!"

"Well, let's say 'borrow.' I want you to 'borrow' some potatoes from the fields."

"But dear, I can't do this," Mr. Yeh replied.

"Oh! But you can let us die of hunger!" his wife shouted.

Then she started to cry as she had never cried before.

And so finally Mr. Yeh agreed to "borrow" some sweet potatoes.

The next evening he took a basket and walked toward the fields. These sweet potato fields belonged to a widow, Liu Sao, and her only son, young Hsiao-pao. Liu Sao knew that New Year's Eve was a good time for people to steal sweet potatoes because she would be busy cooking and couldn't watch her fields. So this year she decided to take her son to the fields to guard the potatoes. She put up a tent for Hsiao-pao to sit in, left him, and went home to continue her work. Hsiao-pao sat silently in the darkness, waiting and listening. He had brought a big stick to beat any thieves with and he felt very serious and brave and strong.

He sat there for hours trying not to fall asleep. Just as his eyes were closing, he heard a small noise. He looked out into the dark night and saw a person walking very quietly along the edge of the field. He couldn't see if it was a man or a woman. He watched and waited. This person then went into the small temple at the edge of the field, where people came to pray to the Buddha of earth. Hsiao-pao went quickly to the temple and hid inside. He saw the person, a man, kneeling in front of the Buddha and whispering. In the darkness Hsiao-pao recognized his old teacher, Mr. Yeh. He was curious to know what Mr. Yeh was saying but he couldn't quite hear, so he moved very quietly nearer to the Buddha.

He heard Mr. Yeh asking, "Buddha, what should I do?" Then Mr. Yeh told the Buddha what had happened to him and how his wife now wanted him to "borrow" some sweet potatoes. He asked if the Buddha thought it was all right to do this "just once" because of their money problems. "If you think this is all right, please show me," he prayed.

Then he stood up, took some *ch'ien* out of their box near the Buddha, threw them on the ground, closed his eyes and prayed. *Chi'en* are sticks that show your future. People use them to ask the gods for advice when they don't know what to do. The *chi'en* have long and short lines cut into each side. You throw the sticks on the ground and read the pattern they make. Different patterns have different meanings. One of the patterns means "yes."

Hsiao-pao laughed to himself when he heard what Mr. Yeh was praying about.

"I think I'll pretend to be Buddha tonight and have some fun," he thought.

So while Mr. Yeh was praying, Hsiao-pao moved closer and looked at the sticks. They didn't make the "yes" pattern, but he quickly changed the pattern so that they did.

Mr. Yeh opened his eyes, looked at the sticks and smiled.

"Oh, thank you, Buddha," he cried. "I promise to live well and pay Liu Sao and her son back as soon as I get some money."

He kissed the ground at the Buddha's feet three times and left the temple.

Hsiao-pao quietly followed him, laughing to himself and thinking about how his old teacher, Mr. Yeh, had always told his students never to steal. He hid behind some bushes at the edge of the field and watched Mr. Yeh fill his basket with sweet potatoes that he dug from the earth. As Hsiao-pao watched, he thought, "Mr. Yeh was an excellent teacher but he's terrible at digging!"

Mr. Yeh was so inexperienced and afraid of being discovered that he dug very slowly. He finally cried out, "This is hopeless! Please help me, Buddha!"

Hsiao-pao felt very sympathetic about poor Mr. Yeh's situation. "You want some help?" he thought. "I'll help and have some more fun at the same time."

He took out his knife and started digging up sweet potatoes. He could do this very quickly because he was so experienced. As soon as he had gathered several potatoes on the ground around him, he threw a handful at Mr. Yeh.

"Ouch!" Mr. Yeh, said, as one hit his head. "Oh, Buddha, thank you!"

The potatoes continued to rain down all around him as Hsiao-pao threw them from behind the bushes. Mr. Yeh was amazed. He thanked Buddha again but asked him to slow down a little. When Hsiao-pao, the little Buddha, thought that Mr. Yeh had enough, he stopped. Mr. Yeh then finished filling his basket and walked slowly home.

Liu Sao finished her cooking and came to get her son. She was very angry when she found the tent empty, holes everywhere and many of her sweet potatoes gone.

"Look at this mess!" she shouted. "Did you fall asleep? Where are my sweet potatoes?"

"Mr. Yeh stole them, Mother!" Hsiao-pao told her with excitement.

"Hsiao-pao! Don't say such things about your old teacher, who is such a good man and has helped so many people!"

Hsiao-pao cried, "But it's true, mother, and I helped him!"

Then he told her the whole story. Liu Sao felt sorry for Mr. Yeh and realized that he must be having a difficult time. So she decided that the next morning she and Hsiao-pao would go and wish Mr. Yeh and his wife a happy New Year, and take them some of the delicious New Year's food that she had cooked.

The next morning, as Liu Sao and Hsiao-pao were walking up to Mr. Yeh's house, they heard Mr. and Mrs. Yeh talking happily to each other. They stood under the window to listen and were very surprised to hear what they were saying.

"Old woman, help yourself, eat some lovely pork with red wine."

"Old man, don't be shy, have some nice cold sliced pork."

Hsiao-pao was very upset. "He lied! He's a thief! He stole our sweet potatoes but all the time he had money to buy pork!"

"Quiet, son," his mother said, and she looked through the window to see what was happening. She saw Mr. Yeh putting a piece of red-skinned sweet potato into his wife's bowl as she was putting a piece of white-skinned sweet potato into his bowl. They were both pretending that they were eating real pork!

"It's all right, son," she said.

Then she lifted Hsiao-pao up so he could see. He immediately jumped down, banged on Mr. Yeh's door and shouted for him to come.

When Mr. Yeh heard Hsiao-pao, he jumped up from his chair, frightened, and whispered to his wife, "Oh no! Hsiao-pao's here! Quick! Hide these!"

Mrs. Yeh quickly took away the rest of the potatoes while Mr. Yeh looked for a place to hide the skins of the potatoes they had already eaten. He rushed to the fire, put them in a pot and put the lid on. Then he opened the door for Hsiao-pao and his mother.

"Happy New Year, Mr. Yeh," said Liu Sao, as she gave him his New Year's Eve food.

Mr. Yeh was very embarrassed, but before he could say anything A-ken Sao came through the door with her daughter, Ying-hua.

"Mr. Yeh," A-ken Sao called. "We've just come to thank you again for giving us A-ken's money and making our New Year such a happy one. Happy New Year to you and your good wife."

While all this was happening, no one noticed that A-ken had appeared and was standing in the door listening. So they all jumped when he quietly asked, "What's this about my money?"

"My darling!" cried A-ken Sao, and she rushed into his arms, saying, "I'm just thanking Mr. Yeh for giving me . . ."

"I know, I heard," he answered. "But I didn't give Mr. Yeh anything. I'm completely confused."

Hsiao-Pao suddenly interrupted. "I know everything! Sit down and let me tell you!" And he told them the whole story.

When he had finished, both A-ken and his wife fell down on their knees in front of Mr. Yeh, crying, "Oh, Mr. Yeh, how can we thank you?"

Hsiao-pao laughed loudly then for the first time. He ran over to the pot where Mr. Yeh had hidden the sweet potato skins. He took them out, threw them up in the air and shouted, "Happy New Year!"

ACTIVITIES

The Good Peasant's Son

Before you read

1 Read the Introduction. Then name some folktales from your country that contain characters who are evil, who help the hero to succeed, or who play tricks on other characters.

2 Look at the Word List at the back of the book. Check the meaning of unfamiliar words. Then complete the sentences.

   a The .... was cleaning the bedroom when her employer came in.

   b .... and .... are both birds that hunt and kill other birds.

   c It was very early but the .... were already working in the rice fields.

   d Everyone in the village had gone to the .... to pray.

   e In Russia, people pay with .... In India, they use ....

   f A .... is a creature with sharp teeth that lives in rivers.

   g What would you like to drink, ... or .... ?

   h The .... was as tall as two men.

   i The dress was made of .... and was very beautiful.

   j A .... is a big, round, green or yellow fruit.

While you read

3 Put the events in the correct order. Number them 1–10.

   a Martin's ring is stolen from him and he is imprisoned.   .....
   b Martin saves a girl in a forest.   .....
   c The czar's daughter returns.   .....
   d A mouse gets the ring back.   .....
   e Martin buys a cat.   .....
   f Martin marries the czar's daughter.   .....
   g Martin buys a dog.   .....
   h Martin is given a ring with special powers.   .....

84

i The ring is discovered in a fish. .....

j Martin works for a priest. .....

After you read

4 Answer the questions.

   a Why does Martin's mother send him away?

   b How does Martin save the girl in the forest from the fire?

   c What are the special powers of the ring?

   d How does the czar's daughter succeed in getting the ring?

   e How does the czar punish Martin?

   f How do Jourka and Vaska get the ring from the princess?

   g How does Vaska lose the ring?

5 Give three or four examples of Martin's behavior which show that he is a kind, gentle person who is not interested in money.

6 Discuss whether you think there is a lesson for us in the story. If there is, do you agree with it?

7 Work with another student. Act out a conversation in which Martin explains to a friend why he took back the czar's daughter.

The Crocodile and the Hunter

Before you read

8 Discuss what you know about crocodiles. Do you expect crocodiles in stories to be kind or nasty? Why?

While you read

9 Complete the sentences with one or two words.

   a Boaji asks the hunter to give him some ....

   b The crocodile asks the hunter to take him to the ....

   c The crocodile promises to give the hunter some ....

   d The crocodile pulls the hunter under the ....

   e The mat says that life is not ....

   f The .... and the .... agree with the mat.

   g Boaji asks the crocodile to .... him what happened.

   h The hunter .... to take the crocodile back to the river.

After you read

10 Explain why the mat, the piece of cloth, and the old horse say that life isn't fair.

11 Describe:

    a the crocodile's punishment for his bad behavior.

    b the hunter's reward for his kindness to Boaji.

12 Discuss these questions. Give reasons for your opinions.

    a Do you think the crocodile deserved his treatment by the hunter and Boaji?

    b Do you agree with the last two lines of the story?

13 Work with another student. Act out a conversation in which the hunter describes what happened to him to a friend.

Breaking the Chain

Before you read

14 Read the description of the story in the Introduction (page ix). What might the mandate order the hero of the story to do?

While you read

15 Circle the correct answers.

    a Juanantes is a *good man / man who drinks a lot of alcohol*.

    b Juanantes drinks some whiskey and a voice tells him to go to the top of a mountain and *find / burn* a bag.

    c *Cardenala / Juanantes* wants to do what the voice says.

    d When they find the bag, the mandate in the bag orders Juanantes to *find / kill* a man called Prudencio Salvatierra.

    e When Juanantes meets Prudencio, he *kills / wounds* him.

    f Juanantes goes to prison for *ten / twelve* years.

    g Cardelana *leaves / stays with* Juanantes.

    h The mandate's final order is that Juanantes must give an order to *help / kill* someone.

    i The old man tells Juanantes that he (the old man) fell into the *good / evil* light.

    j Juanantes's mandate is to take the picture of someone with a *good / bad* heart and tear it to pieces.

After you read

16 Complete the sentences.

    a Juanantes kills Prudencio because ....

    b Cardelana leaves Juanantes because ....

    c Juanantes doesn't want to kill again because ....

    d Juanantes knows an evil light is in him because ....

    e The evil light leaves Juanantes because ....

17 Explain why the story is called "Breaking the Chain," and the old man's part in the chain. How does Juanantes succeed in "breaking the chain"?

18 Work with another student. Imagine that Juanantes and Cardenala meet some time after the end of the story. Act out their conversation.

Lukas's Luck

Before you read

19 Below are some words and phrases from the story. What do you think the story will be about?

    poor farmer   baby daughter   christening   godmother

    mayor's wife   poor old woman   gold coin   golden pile

While you read

20 Are the sentences below true (T) or false (F)?

    a Lukas and his wife have always been poor.   .....

    b They want their baby daughter to be christened.   .....

    c The mayor's wife agrees to be their baby daughter's godmother.   .....

    d Lukas meets an old woman.   .....

    e The priest agrees to christen the baby without being paid.   .....

    f The old woman gives Lukas two golden ducats.   .....

    g Lukas and his wife find that they have a lot of money.   .....

    h Lukas becomes rich and wise.   .....

After you read

21 Explain how one ducat is enough to make Lucas and his wife rich.

22 Discuss which of these statements is the most important lesson of the story:

People and things are not always what they seem.

Your luck can change.

Wisdom for Sale

Before you read

23 Read the first paragraph of the story. What do you think might happen in the story?

While you read

24 Complete the sentences with one or two words.

a The boy needs to work because he is an ....

b He opens a store that offers to sell ....

c His first piece of advice is given to a ....

d Two maids fight in the marketplace about a ....

e The queens order the merchant's son to be a ....

f The Brahman boy advises him to pretend to be ....

g The boy advises the king to .... before he does anything.

h The doctor thinks that the king knows that his drink is ....

i The boy becomes the king's new ....

After you read

25 Who says or writes these words and to whom? Explain the situation.

a "It is not wise to stand and watch two people fighting."

b "You must sign a document saying that your son will never use my advice."

c "Excuse me, I didn't push in front of you."

d "When they call you to the palace, pretend to be crazy."

e "It will cost you 100,000 rupees."

f "Forgive me, my king."

26 Work with another student. Act out the conversation in which the merchant's son tells the king the whole story about the melons and the king is amused and forgives him.

The Wooden Horse

Before you read

27 Read the lines in the Introduction on page (??) about "The Wooden Horse." What adventures do you think the young prince might have on the wooden horse?

While you read

28 Put the events in the correct order. Number them 1–8.

a The prince secretly takes the princess to his father's palace.   .....

b The prince and a beautiful princess fall in love.   .....

c A wizard shows the king of Persia what his wooden horse can do.   .....

d The prince says that he can cure the princess of her craziness.   .....

e The wizard escapes with the princess and the horse.   .....

f Prince Kamar Al-Akmar flies far away and lands on the roof of a palace.   .....

g A king in the land of the Greeks puts the wizard in prison.   .....

h The prince and princess marry.   .....

After you read

29 Answer the questions.

a Why doesn't the youngest daughter of Sabur want to marry the wizard?

b Why is the wizard angry with the prince? How does he punish him?

c What does the princess's father say that the prince must do to show his bravery?

d When the prince returns to his own palace, why are the rooms dark and empty?

e Why does the princess pretend to be crazy?

30 Work with another student. Discuss this question: In what way are the Brahmin boy in "Wisdom for Sale" and Prince Kamar Al-Akmar similar?

The Wedding Box

Before you read

31 Discuss situations in which important events have made people you know kinder and less selfish. Compare them with situations in which people haven't taken the opportunity to change.

While you read

32 Are these sentences true (T) or false (F)?

    a Hsiang-ling is easy to please. .....

    b Hsiang-ling is not very interested in the wedding box. .....

    c She gives the box to a rich woman who admires it. .....

    d She loses her house, husband and child in a storm. .....

    e Although she is hungry, she gives her food to an old woman. .....

    f She starts work for a family, taking care of their son. .....

    g She discovers her wedding box. .....

    h Mrs. Lu's husband explains how the wedding box helped him and his wife. .....

    i She finds her husband and child again. .....

After you read

33 Describe Hsiang-Ling's two acts of kindness and how they change her life and other people's lives.

The Golden Apples

Before you read

34 Read the first paragraph of the story. What do you think the story might be about?

While you read

35 Choose the correct answers.

    a Three gods visit the world of *the giants* / *men*.

    b An enormous eagle *gives them* / *eats* all their food.

    c Loki promises the eagle to *kill* / *bring him* the goddess Idun.

    d The giant Thiazi takes Idun to the *Jotunheim* / *sea*.

    e The gods start *quarreling* / *growing old* because they have lost the golden apples.

f Loki changes Idun into a *small stone / falcon* and brings her back to Asgard.

g *The eagle / Loki* is burned in an enormous fire.

h The gods eat the golden apples and *become young again / ask Loki to leave.*

After you read

36 Describe these characters:

  a Loki   **b** Idun   **c** Thiazi   **d** Odun

37 Read the final paragraph of the story again. What does it tell us about the world of the gods?

Happy New Year

Before you read

38 Is New Year an important time in your country? How do you celebrate it? What do you know about how the Chinese celebrate New Year?

While you read

39 Answer the questions. Who:

  a is waiting for a husband to return after he has been away for almost a year?   .....
  b is afraid that she may have to sell her daughter?   .....
  c gives A-ken Sao a silver *yüan-pao*?   .....
  d tells Mr. Yeh to "borrow" some sweet potatoes?   .....
  e sees Mr. Yeh by the edge of the sweet potato field?   .....
  f throws sweet potatoes at Mr. Yeh?   .....
  g visits Mr. Yeh with some delicious New Year's food?   .....
  h thank Mr. Yeh for his great kindness?   .....

After you read

40 There are three acts of kindness by different people in this story. Describe these acts of kindness and the reason for them.

41 Work with another student. Discuss this question. Why was New Year's Eve a bad time to borrow money in China at that time? What do people in your country believe can bring bad luck at particular times?

Writing

42 Imagine that a magazine has asked the Brahman boy in "Wisdom for Sale" to write about his experiences, with the title "My Story." Begin like this: *After the flood, I lost my parents and I had no food, no money, nowhere to live. I had to do something. ...*

43 Write a page from Juanantes's diary, when he is in prison, after he realizes that he is losing Cardenala.

44 Say whether you agree with the statement "Folktales teach us important lessons about life." Give reasons from your opinion. Give also examples from folktales in this collection and from your own country's folktales.

45 Write a letter from Hsiang-ling to her mother after she begins working for Yüan-wai Lu. In it she tells her mother what has happened to her, apologizes for her past behavior, and thanks her.

46 Write a description of one of the characters from these stories who you think is wise, clever, or silly. Give examples of their behavior to explain your opinion. Then compare them with a person you know.

47 Write about your favorite story in this collection, saying why you liked it. Did it make you think?

48 Compare two folktales in this collection. Explain how they are similar, giving examples, and how they are different.

49 Write a letter from Martin to his mother ("The Good Peasant's Son"). The letter is written after Martin has won back the czarevna and his palace. In the letter Martin explains what happened to him and the ring after he married the czarevna.

50 Write a book report on this collection of folktales. Give short descriptions of each folktale and say whether you think they are interesting and enjoyable, and why.

51 Choose a folktale from your own culture and write the story.

WORD LIST

butcher (n) someone who owns or works in a store that sells meat

christen (v) to name a child and make them a member of the Christian church in a religious ceremony soon after birth

claw (n) a sharp, hard, curved part on the toe of an animal or bird

crocodile (n) a large animal with a long body and a long mouth with sharp teeth that lives in hot, wet areas

duck (n) a common water bird with short legs that is used for its meat, eggs and soft feathers

eagle (n) a large wild bird that eats small animals and birds

falcon (n) a large bird that is often trained to hunt small animals

giant (n) a person, especially in stories, who is very tall, big, and strong

godmother (n) a woman who promises, usually in a religious ceremony, to help a child by teaching them religious values

jade (n) a stone, usually green, used for making jewelry

machete (n) a large knife with a broad, heavy blade

maid (n) a female servant

mandate (n) an instruction to do something

mat (n) a small piece of thick material that covers part of a floor

mayor (n) someone who is elected to lead the government of a town or city

melon (n) a large, sweet, juicy fruit with a hard skin and flat seeds

merchant (n) someone who buys and sells large quantities of goods

peasant (n) someone who does farm work on the small piece of land where they live

prime minister (n) the leader of the government in countries that have a parliament

rouble (n) Russian money

rupee (n) Indian money

silk (n) soft, fine cloth made from a substance produced by a kind of small animal

spirit (n) a living thing without a physical body, like a ghost

tale (n) a story about imaginary or exciting events; a **folktale** is a story which is traditional to the ordinary people in an area; a **fairy tale**

is a story for children, involving imaginary creatures and magical events

temple (n) a building where people go to pray in some religions

terrify (v) to make someone extremely afraid

treasure (n) gold, silver, jewels, and other valuable objects

vodka (n) a strong, clear alcoholic drink

whiskey (n) a strong alcoholic drink made from grain

wizard (n) a man who is believed to have special magic powers